It's Always Too Soon To Quit

Lewis R. Timberlake

Fleming H. Revell
Old Tappan, New Jersey

Library of Congress Cataloging-in-Publication Data

Timberlake, Lewis.
  It's always too soon to quit / Lewis Timberlake.
    p. cm.
  Bibliography: p.
  ISBN 0-8007-1596-9
  1. Success. 2. Christian life—1960–   I. Title.
BJ1611.2.T565 1988
248.4—dc19   88-11470
                                                 CIP

Copyright © 1988 by Lewis Timberlake
Published by the Fleming H. Revell Company
Old Tappan, New Jersey 07675
Printed in the United States of America

To

Jackie and Troy, who lost their daughter when she
was only seven and who have taught me that love
never dies and faith is sufficient.

Drayton, whose enthusiasm for life and dedication
to his goals have taught me that eagles fly above
the storm clouds to greatness.

Tom, who saw me at my lowest, believed in me
when he didn't have to, and is a testimony to the
goodness of man and the greatness of God.

Bruce, who lost his brother in the prime of life and
who has taught me dignity in despair and courage
in crisis.

And, finally, my children:
Brad and Julie,
Terry and Terri,
and Craig
whose unqualified love and undying confidence remind me
daily that it's always too soon to quit!

Acknowledgments

I am grateful to the following people whose contributions made this book possible:

Marietta Reed, who continues to impress me with her talent and professionalism. Her writing ability has made it possible for my thoughts and ideas to be transformed into the written word.

Jim Caldwell, Allen Clark, Sharon Echols, and T George Harris, who have generously allowed me to share their stories—stories that illustrate well how a person can learn from and grow through the tough times in life.

Brad Timberlake, whose insightful editing and valuable ideas and suggestions have contributed significantly to the content of this book.

And, finally, the many authors and publishers who graciously permitted me to quote from their material.

Contents

Foreword

It's Always Too Soon to Quit is a message whose time has come. I have to, in all candor, confess that I would have said the same things a hundred years ago, had I been around, and would write them again a hundred years from now if I were going to be here. The truths and principles Lewis Timberlake expounds in this book are simply a tribute to the fact that the indomitable will of man, when supported by the love and power of God, can overcome obstacles that surround and overwhelm people with less commitment and without a personal relationship with our Lord.

Story after story, example after example, illustration after illustration all give credence to the fact that there was much truth in what Bach said when he observed that there are only three great things in this world—an ocean, a mountain, and a dedicated man. Once man has made his commitment and starts utilizing his resources and applying his initiative, energy, and enthusiasm, while claiming the unlimited power of almighty God, then those mountains do move into the sea, and obstacles that seemed insurmountable begin to wither and fall away.

It's Always Too Soon to Quit is fascinating, interesting, on occasion humorous, and oftentimes downright inspiring. It convinces us that we can, teaches us how, motivates us to do, and inspires us to reach for higher rungs on the ladder. Easy to read and ideal to pick up for a brief respite from the day's activities or to snuggle up with for an afternoon or evening of old-fashioned inspiration. I recommend it for young and old alike.

Zig Ziglar

Introduction

My travels take me all over the continent and sometimes beyond and put me in contact with people from almost every walk of life. From every corner of our society I hear four words spoken more often today than any other phrase: "Is there any hope?" I'm asked that question by people from all walks of life, rich and poor, young and old, black and white, male and female, married and single.

I realize that it's a tough world we live in. At some time in our lives we each must face despair, whether it be the loss of a job, the death of a loved one, the breakup of a marriage, or unbearable financial burdens. There are times in a person's life when he wakes up and realizes that he's not the success he'd always planned to be. Problems seem to pile upon problems, worries upon worries, and fear begins to dominate his life. Tears flow more frequently. Sleep comes less easily. And he may begin to wonder why God doesn't seem to care, if God is really listening, or if God is even there at all.

I know these feelings because I've been there, too. I've known great days when I could hardly wait to get up so that I could enjoy the challenge and opportunity of making things happen. On the other hand, I've experienced desperate times as well. I've known days when sleep would not come, days when I had to fight to hold back the tears, and days when I wasn't sure I could meet the payroll or pay the bills. There have been times when I wasn't certain that I was loved or cared for and times when I questioned if God was near or if God was even real. Those are the tough times in life, the testing times in life.

Maybe you've been there as well. If you haven't, you will

11

be. History tells us that every person, at some point in life, must look into the dark valley. Maybe you feel that you're in just as much trouble as the people you hear about. Perhaps you've lost your job or are going through financial difficulties. Maybe you've lost a loved one or have problems with a troubled child. Or perhaps you were born with a birth defect or have experienced a devastating illness or injury that has left you permanently disabled. Maybe in desperation you've turned to drugs or alcohol and can't seem to get out from under your oppressive burden. There may have been a time when you wanted to run away or actually contemplated suicide.

I've learned that everyone must face his or her own Gethsemane. Everyone must come to a point of testing—a time that can make a person either *bitter* or *better*. When some people reach this point they simply accept defeat and give up; others refuse to allow the tough times to defeat them and persevere to overcome their difficulties. How can you get up when you've been knocked down? What can you do when all hope seems lost? Why do some people manage to turn their problems into possibilities? Why do some seem to grow through the tough times, learn from them, and overcome overwhelming odds to step back on the path of success, happiness, and hope?

I believe the answers to these questions lie in one simple, yet basic, truth: **It's always too soon to quit!** Whether you emerge from trouble a better person or a bitter person depends not on what happens to you, but how you react to what happens to you. I hope to prove this truth to you by sharing stories of people who have faced defeat, despair, and discouragement. Each of these re- markable people seems to deeply and fervently believe that *failure is never final.* Their stories tell of courageous people who have been knocked down, but refused to stay down—who have been willing to dream great dreams, take grest risks, suffer great hurts, and yet rebound to great heights. You can draw strength from these wonder- ful people, learn from them, and—I hope—be inspired to become like them.

Introduction

I want you to find the faith and courage to persevere in the tough times. I want to share steps by which you can make your own "breaks" in life and enjoy success in everything you do. And after reading this book, I sincerely hope that you will be able to draw strength and comfort from the knowledge of a living and loving God. He is a source of unconditional love, uncompromising acceptance, and unlimited power—power that can lift you up out of your valley, bring you through the tough times, and set you on the path of hope.

Finally, it is my fondest wish that someday *you* will be one of the people I tell stories about—people who never gave up their hope or lost their courage, people who have faith in themselves, in God, and in the truth that it's always too soon to quit!

God loves you, and so do I!

LEWIS TIMBERLAKE

Part One

Two Truths
to
Live By

1

It's Always
Too Soon to Quit!

As we reach milestones in our lives, we characteristically pause and look at where we've been and where we might be going. As we grow into adulthood, our youthful naivete is often replaced by cynicism, discontent, and distrust. Each generation, like those that have gone before, must learn to face death, illness, divorce, financial stress, and so on. These problems aren't new—only the realization that they are very present and very, very real.

John Greenleaf Whittier wrote, "The saddest words of tongue and pen are simply these: 'It might have been.'" I think that all of us have felt this way at one time or another. But, implicit in Mr. Whittier's statement is that this feeling is final. I believe that some of the most *exciting* words are "it might have been, except for. . . ." There have been many people who didn't allow the thought to end with "it might have been." They pressed on, using the principles laid out in this book, and created an entirely new ending.

How to Get to California—Method #1

A small boy born in Harlem, New York, in 1921 was frequently left with relatives so his vaudevillian parents

17

could go on tour. His mean, abusive mother often vented her vicious temper on her young son. During his childhood he stayed with dozens of alcoholic aunts and uncles who deposited him in eighteen different schools before he finally graduated from high school. At age thirteen he ran away from home to seek an aunt in California, riding his bicycle most of the way until it broke down. He continued his journey on freight trains, eating ant-covered leftovers that wandering hoboes had left behind.

After a short term in the army, he began a radio career in the late forties and went on to other radio shows and finally to television. He has since written two poetry anthologies, two short story collections, and several novels. Also an accomplished pianist and lyricist, he has written over four thousand songs, including scores for Broadway plays. In addition, he is a popular lecturer and wrote the "Meeting of the Minds" series for PBS television. But, perhaps Steve Allen is best known for creating the format for late-night television, the comedic talk show he created in 1953 and which first went on the air in 1954 as "The Tonight Show."

Sooner or later, all of us have to live through an extremely difficult time—a disabling illness or injury, the loss of a loved one, a broken heart, the loss of a job, financial difficulties, drug or alcohol dependency, troubled children. This is the time when we question whether or not life is still worth living. Is the dream worth the price? This is the time when hope flees our hearts, when fear paralyzes our minds and destroys our enthusiasm, and when tears rush to our eyes more often than laughter to our lips.

When we reach this low point in life, worship no longer lifts our spirits and prayer seems useless. This is the time when we question everything we ever believed in. We even question God's love for us, sometimes wondering if we still believe in God at all. This is the winter season of the soul, the dark night of the heart, the testing hour of the spirit. This is when many people throw up their hands in despair and simply give up and quit.

Many of us look in envy at famous and successful people—people like Steve Allen who've "made it"—and say, "I could have done that if I'd been in his shoes. He had all the right breaks. I could be successful, too, if times weren't so tough and I could just get some breaks in my life." We look at the supposedly greener grass in our neighbor's yard and use the hard times we've been through to justify why we aren't as successful as they are. In truth, if we could take everyone's problems and put them in a pile and then pick out the ones we would want for ourselves, we'd probably pick our own. When we look in envy at others' successes, their lives seem glamorous. But, when we look at their failures and other problems, our own begin to take on a new perspective.

Steve Allen overcame a childhood of abuse, rejection, bitterness, and loneliness and strove to become more than he was. He made a conscious decision to change his circumstances. And in his quest to better himself, he developed a deep love for the underdog and the oppressed, surpassed only by his compassionate and undying sense of humor. His life serves as an example to us all. He knows the first truth that I would like to share with you: *It's always too soon to quit!*

Statistics show that only 10 percent of the population actually "succeed" at what they set out to accomplish. Another 10 percent accept defeat and turn to a variety of things while seeking a solution to their anger and desperation—alcohol, drugs, living on the streets, prostitution, the occult, and even suicide. The balance, who make up 80 percent of the population, simply "endure." These are the people who have dreams they feel will never be accomplished, jobs they don't like but feel they can do nothing about, and so on. They live out their lives in frustration because they feel the tough times they have experienced prevented them from getting the right breaks in life.

In reality, we don't fail because we don't get any breaks. We fail because we don't accept responsibility for our mistakes and learn from our experiences. We fail because we don't take decisive actions that will do something about our predicament. We fail because we turn away from God and don't allow Him to have control of our lives. And we fail because we roll over, accept defeat, give up, and quit too soon.

Many people feel that abortion is wrong because it snuffs out the life of one of God's creations before it even has a chance to live. Yet, some of these same people will "abort" their own lives by giving up and quitting when things get rough. The times when life seems darkest and people feel the most forsaken are the times we have the opportunity to prove our true worth. The successful people in life, the people who overcome adversity and rise from the ashes of defeat to rebuild their lives into something positive and fruitful, are the people who refuse to give up, refuse to quit. You can become a part of the 10 percent who make it! You can't control what life hands you, but you can control how you react to your life's circumstances.

How to Get to California—Method #2

A young Texan girl's family was forced to live with her grandparents during the Depression because her father couldn't find work. She slept in a bed with four other relatives and survived by eating jackrabbit caught on the Texas plains. Her family moved to California when she was seven and it was there that she spent the rest of her life. At age sixteen she won the Miss Burbank contest—an event that led to a part in a movie.

As an adult, her first marriage ended in a bitter divorce so she raised her two children alone. Her second marriage to a millionaire shoe manufacturer ended when his financial gambles caused the failure of his business and left her with millions of dollars in debts to repay. The banks repossessed everything, including her home. But, determined to pay back her debts and properly care for her family, she went on the road doing live theater. It took her over ten years, working forty weeks per year, to pay back the millions in debts with which her ex-husband had burdened her. But, the point is, she did it!

Now out of debt, and with her current home paid for, Debbie Reynolds can look back with pride over a thirty-five-year career in show business. She has appeared in dozens of films, won gold records for several recorded songs, and has her own best-selling exercise video. She is still busy working in theater, managing a dance studio, promoting her exercise video, and working on a new television series.

Was Debbie Reynolds in the right place at the right time? Did she simply get the "breaks" in life? No. Of course not. She says the secret to her success is the fact that she *believes* she can survive. She keeps getting up after she falls and refuses to quit. That belief, along with her faith and her sense of humor, has seen Debbie Reynolds through some very tough times. She also knows that it's always too soon to quit.

Successful people accept responsibility for their mistakes and learn from their experiences. They make conscious decisions and take action to effect change in their lives and triumph over their difficulties. And successful people don't give up and quit. Anyone can quit. That's the easy way out.

Entertainer Dolly Parton comes from a poor Appalachian family of nineteen children. A fan in her TV audience once asked her why she became successful when so many other poor mountain people did not.

"I never stopped trying," she said. "And I never tried stopping."

Trouble can leave you *bitter* or it can leave you *better*. The choice is up to you. The words of Ella Wheeler Wilcox express it best: "The world is round, and the place that seems like the end may only be the beginning." Sometimes what we think are the worst things that can happen turn out to be the best things for us in the long run.

How to Get to California—Method #3

Several years ago I spoke to a group at the Ritz-Carlton Hotel in Chicago. I had another speech scheduled in San

Diego the following morning. I had one hour from the end of my Chicago speech to get to the airport in time for my flight to California. If I missed that flight, it would be four hours before I could get another. That meant I would get there the following morning, fatigued from lack of sleep. I would have to go before a group of people and exude enthusiasm in an unrefreshed condition. So catching my flight was extremely important to me.

As I crawled into a waiting cab, I told the cabbie I'd give him an extra five dollars if he could get me to the airport on time. He snaked his way through the downtown traffic and onto the freeway at the outskirts of town. So far, so good. Then we came upon an accident that had all the lanes blocked. Cars and trucks were backed up for what seemed like miles. The cabbie tried and tried to ease his way through the sea of glass and metal. Eventually a lane cleared and a uniformed policeman waved the traffic through—traffic that crawled at a snail's pace. My impatience grew with every second.

Once we eased into a clear lane, the cabbie shoved his right foot to the floorboard. Trees, cars, and buildings zipped by the windows in a blur. Finally, we pulled up to the main entrance of the airport terminal where I jumped out of the car, grabbed my luggage, and sped toward my assigned gate. As I arrived and handed my ticket to the agent, he informed me that my plane had just taxied down the runway.

I stood there and got mad at the world—at the cab driver for making me late, at the city of Chicago for its traffic congestion, at the ticket agent for not holding the plane for me, and at anyone who crossed my path at that moment. *I'm a good man,* I thought. *I go to church every Sunday. I even teach Sunday school. I've been happily married to the same woman for thirty-three years, raised three wonderful children, built a successful business from the ground up. Why did this have to happen to me? Now I have to wait four hours for the next flight only to arrive in San Diego too tired and unprepared to give a speech.* As I stood there wallowing in self-pity and anger, I watched my plane take off into the sky . . . then I watched it turn, take a steep nosedive, and crash into the ground.

Trouble isn't always trouble. We experience adversity and setbacks for a purpose, even if we don't know what that purpose is at the time. Our reactions to our circumstances and the choices we make are more important than what happens to us. We can choose to moan, "Oh, I'm just a failure, a nobody, a loser. I can't do anything right. Nothing ever seems to go my way." Or we can choose to examine our lives, look for a positive purpose in our circumstances, and take specific steps that will set us on the path to a better and happier life. The choice is ours.

How to Get From the Field to the Fairway

Calvin Peete grew up in the farm country of central Florida where he and his family made a living picking vegetables. Like any other youth, Calvin had a dream. He wanted to be a professional golfer. His friends laughed at his dream, pointing out that poor blacks just didn't become professional golfers.

In the eighth grade, Calvin found it necessary to drop out of school and go into the fields to help his family earn a living. But, in spite of his daily labor, he always felt God intended more for him than picking vegetables. His dream of becoming a professional golfer would not die, and Calvin took up the game as an adult. He knew it would take a lot of work to turn his dream into a reality, but he was willing to pay the price.

Not only did Calvin have the disadvantage of beginning golf at a late age, but he had to play with a left arm that wouldn't straighten out to full extension—the result of a broken elbow when he was a child. Professional golfers would say it's impossible to play golf without an extended left arm. But Calvin compensated for that disability and within six months he was shooting below eighty. Eighteen months later he was shooting below par and joined the mini-tour in Florida in 1972. In 1975 he qualified for the

PGA tour—the oldest rookie ever at age thirty-five. He won the Greater Milwaukee Open in 1979 and again in 1982 when he became the winningest golfer on the tour. Calvin's persistent belief that God had a plan for his life enabled him to persevere without giving up.

"It's been a long road from the fields to the fairways," Calvin says. "One a lot of people said was impossible from the beginning. But you see, I knew something maybe they didn't. That God had a plan for me—but I had to be willing to work at it. When you work hard and pray hard you have a combination that can take you places you've never imagined. It's taken me from green beans to a putting green . . . and far, far beyond."[1]

When a grain of sand gets inside the oyster's shell, wounding the oyster in the process, the oyster secretes a liquid that coats the sand to protect the oyster from further damage. But, in the meantime, the oyster must go through the pain process before the result—a priceless pearl (and relief from pain)—can be achieved. Besides cleaning the ocean's floor, the oyster doesn't make any impact on life until it provides a food source for man or yields its treasure to the world. It accomplishes *nothing* worthwhile *unless* it gets hurt first!

Just as steel gains its strength only after being sent through the fiery furnace, and just as coal turns into diamonds only after centuries of pressure and friction, so people can, and do, become stronger through the testings and trials of life. You wouldn't be the person you are today without all the experiences (including the trials) you've encountered along life's path.

It's never too late to rise above the ashes. Perhaps we can learn from Paul Harvey. When asked the secret to his success, Mr. Harvey replied, "Every time I fell down, I got up again."

Niccolò Paganini was one of the most beloved and recognized violinists of his time. His gift for music became apparent when he received his first violin lessons from his father, an amateur musician. He made his first public appearance at age nine and his virtuosity soon became legendary throughout Europe. Known for taking the technique of violin playing far beyond its limits, Paganini drew audiences from all over the continent.

As he played at one such concert, demonstrating his genius with his instrument, the crowd grew close, caught up in the magic of his music. As Paganini ingeniously built his song to its climax, one of his violin strings suddenly snapped. The audience gasped, afraid that the concert would most certainly have to end. Paganini continued to play. The audience had no sooner breathed a sigh of relief when a second string snapped. A blanket of silence again fell over the audience. Paganini played on.

Finally, just before the final few notes sounded, the third string of the violin broke. Only one string remained. The audience sat in astonished disbelief as Niccolò Paganini finished the concert with only one string left on his violin. The moment he stopped playing the audience rushed to their feet, cheering wildly and shouting, "Bravo! Bravo!" They knew they had just witnessed a genius at his best.

It's always too soon to quit. No matter what life brings our way, the show must go on—with or without us. And the sooner we learn to get up after the fall, the better persons we will all become.

How to Get From Down to Up

Of the thousands of ways for the animal kingdom to reproduce, the birth of the baby giraffe is to me the most impressive. The mother giraffe gives birth standing up! It seems that the small calf would get hurt from the long fall from its mother's hindquarters, nearly six feet above the hard ground. Within seconds after giving birth, the mother rolls the calf over into an upright position with its legs tucked under its body. She then swings an enormous leg outward and actually kicks her new baby so that it's sent sprawling head over hooves. She wants it to get up, and if it doesn't, she'll repeat the same procedure until it does.

The struggle to rise is momentous. And as the baby tires of trying, the mother will continue to stimulate its efforts with hefty kicks. You see, she wants the baby to *remember* how it got up so it can get up quickly from that point on. In the wild, animals need to get up as soon as possible after birth in order to follow the protective herd and escape their predators. The mother needs to teach the baby to rise quickly and get on with its short life.

What a lesson this is. How many great moments in a person's life come only after a time of testing? Successful people (whether economically, spiritually, emotionally, socially, physically, or intellectually successful) are those who are able to get up after the fall and try again. They know that by getting up and persevering they can learn from the tough times and make their own breaks in life. They can ensure their own success. This never-give-up *attitude* enables many people who encounter problems, both big and small, to look for solutions.

In 1969, magazine editor T George Harris took a little-known magazine, put it in the black, and made it one of the outstanding magazines of its time. In 1976, soon after his magazine was bought out by a major chain, Harris learned that his wife had breast cancer. Eight months later he lost his job as magazine editor. He then watched the magazine he had worked so hard to build suffer hard times and slowly decline until it was ultimately sold at a giveaway price.

At age fifty-five he found himself alone (his wife was by then in Sloan-Kettering Hospital), out of work, and with four children to clothe and feed. He began growing vegetables in his backyard to help feed his family and took occasional carpentry jobs to earn a little money. But Harris says the most significant part of his struggle was taking over the responsibilities of a working "mother." His sons helped him run the house and shared in the chores. He purchased a gross of white athletic socks and a gross of maroon socks so he wouldn't have to "sort and match" the laundry—he'd just leave a basket of socks on the stairs.

"Maroon is a universal color," he says. "It goes just as

badly with blue, gray, and black as with brown and green."

Harris couldn't afford taxis, so he began jogging to and from free-lance jobs and then to the hospital to be with his wife during her meals. He gave up junk food and that, along with his daily jogging, resulted in a weight loss of thirty pounds. His hectic schedule continued for months. Some evenings he wouldn't get home until nine or ten. Then in January 1978 his wife died of cancer.

Harris's busy schedule continued for four more years. In 1982 the combination of his improved health, his struggle to survive, and his will to succeed led him to take a risk. With little money, he and a partner launched a new magazine from a seedy office in New York City. In a few short years, *American Health* has attracted a circulation approaching a million subscribers and has received a National Magazine award. T George Harris obviously didn't get "the breaks." *He made his own breaks.*

When asked how he kept calm during the tough times, Harris said he simply kept repeating the prayer, "Not my will, Lord, but Thine," over and over again.

Successful people don't give up and quit. We can't allow any setback, whether large or small, to defeat us. It's just as important to conquer the little day-by-day obstacles as it is to conquer the larger ones. That's how you can make a difference in life.

Got a Lemon, Make Lemonade—Got a Waffle . . .

A young waffle vendor at the 1904 St. Louis World's Fair ran out of the cardboard plates on which he served waffles covered with ice cream. No other vendors at the fair would sell him enough plates to replenish his supply. So that evening the vendor went home and, with the help of his wife, made a batch of one thousand waffles. He then placed them on the ironing board and proceeded to press each one with a flat iron. While they were still hot, he rolled each flattened waffle into a circular shape resembling a cone. As the waffles cooled, they became hard, retaining their conical shape.

The next morning a very sleepy waffle vendor opened for business as usual and sold ice cream in the new waffle cones. Before noon, he had sold all the waffles and all his ice cream! This creative man refused to accept defeat because of a small setback—a setback, I might add, that could have cost him a lot of money in those days. And as a result of the stumbling block of running out of plates, he invented the ice-cream cone!

The waffle vendor was just as successful as Steve Allen, Debbie Reynolds, Calvin Peete, and T George Harris because he achieved his ultimate goal. Success for one may not be success for another. But it is always achieved through perseverance and a determination not to let any setback, major or minor, deter you from your purpose.

• Mary Crowley, the late founder of Home Interiors and author of *Women Who Win,* defined success in this way: "Success is doing what God wants you to do and doing it with a commitment to excellence. . . . Success is a moving target. When you're a young mother with little children, success [may be] coping with the day, filling the children's needs, being a wife to your husband, and managing things around the house. When the children are in school . . . then perhaps you might have a part-time career. Success then [may] be doing that well at that time in your life. Then, when the children are grown and gone from home, you [might] take on a full-time career . . . Success moves as we grow in life."[2]

• Joe Carcione also knows that success is defined differently for each person. He, too, knows that we must each determine what our own dreams are and work for them. Carcione spent most of his life around produce, beginning as a teenager working in a produce terminal in San Francisco. Twenty-five years later he started his own produce company which later went into bankruptcy after his accountant siphoned off $150,000 from the business.

But, yearning to stay in the produce business that he loved and refusing to give up and quit, Carcione fell back on his radio program and newspaper column which gave consumers tips on how to buy quality produce. He has since expanded them into a syndicated television show known as "The Greengrocer" that is viewed by over 7 million Americans in sixty-five cities across the nation.

"Let me tell you something," Carcione says. "The American Dream [success] is as true today as when it attracted our forefathers. It is the freedom to grow as much as we're able. It's the opportunity to rise up when we are flat on our backs and begin again. And it works best when we concentrate on our God-given talents. Mine is to tell people about radishes and cauliflowers. Yours may be being a housewife, typing letters, or helping build houses. But when we concentrate on the *giving* and the *trusting,* it puts us in the best position to reap His blessings."[3]

• After many unhappy and sometimes unsuccessful years working in the "fast lane" as an entertainer's agent, Wally "Famous" Amos renewed his relationship with the Lord and looked to something that had given him pleasure and comfort since childhood—his Aunt Della's chocolate chip cookies. He gave up his career in show business and opened a little cookie shop in Hollywood to sell the cookies he'd been giving away for years. As he baked cookies in preparation for his store opening, Amos prayed and thanked God for allowing him to do something that felt so good and so right and for showing him that his biggest gift was the little things he did for others.

"God gives all of us a special way of getting pleasure," Amos says. "Something that connects the brain and the hands and the personality. Could be gardening or tinkering or a touch at the piano. Or needlepoint or high-rising biscuits or planning a party. The important thing is not to pooh-pooh it because it isn't a big deal or impressive in the eyes of the world. You should never miss out on your calling, or the fun of being *you*."[4]

• Bruce Brookshire, chairman of the board and chief executive officer of the Brookshire Grocery Company in

Tyler, Texas, defines success and successful people in the following way: "Success is something that every person desires, but it rarely, if ever, comes to us by chance or accident. Rather, success is a quality that must be interwoven into every aspect of our lives. In general, successful people share a number of important characteristics.

1. Successful people possess *honesty and integrity*.
2. Successful people are *dedicated to excellence* in anything they do. They are willing to accept nothing less than 100 percent from themselves.
3. Successful people have *determination and tenacity*. They are not discouraged by setbacks, and once they commit to a goal, they stick with it until that goal is accomplished.
4. Successful people are *disciplined*. They are willing to sacrifice the little things in life in order to achieve the things that really count.
5. Successful people have a *positive attitude*. Their thoughts and actions are always of a positive and successful nature.
6. Successful people have *initiative*. When they see that something needs to be done, they don't assume someone else will handle it. They see that it gets done!
7. Successful people are *enthusiastic*. They enjoy what they do, and their exuberant outlook shows through in everything they do.
8. Successful people are *concerned about others*. A truly successful individual will plant the seeds of success in those with whom he or she comes into contact. They care about the welfare and accomplishments of those around them.
9. Successful people have *confidence*. They are not fearful of the future, but instead look to tomorrow with hope and optimism.
10. Successful people have the *ability to dream*. They dream of bigger successes, of new areas in which to achieve success, of how they will achieve those successes, and of how they can benefit their fellowman through their successes.

11. Successful people have *faith in God*. They know that only through His infinite wisdom, strength, and guidance can they overcome the obstacles they will encounter on the road to success.[5]

You will notice that material wealth was not mentioned here as a measure for success. Successful people are those who set goals and work toward them, refuse to give up when setbacks occur, exude an enthusiasm about life and work, trust in God to help them, are hopeful and not fearful, and dare to accomplish all they *want* to accomplish—whatever that may be.

A Dream That Will Not Die

On September 1, 1985, the *Titanic* was discovered nearly three miles deep in the cold North Atlantic Ocean, 350 miles southeast of Newfoundland. For nearly seventy-five years the ship had been celebrated only in legend. Now her massive broken body, tarnished and twisted by years of rust, sediment, and erosion still emitted an aura of haunting elegance and beauty. She rested alone and silent with the scars of the impact with the iceberg that ended her maiden voyage still evident on her side.

Until 1985, men could only guess at the *Titanic*'s whereabouts. But a certain man consumed by a dream couldn't forget her. He had spent thirteen years dominated by his quest to find her. When he finally caught his first glimpse on September 1, he was so fascinated by the majestic ship that he took 53,500 photographs, studying every foot of her gigantic frame. And he was so captured and moved by her that he left the ship undisturbed and unexploited and the final home for 1,522 people who had thought her to be unsinkable.

Dr. Robert Ballard wrote of his find that his first view of the *Titanic* lasted less than two minutes. But the stark sight of her immense black hull would remain forever ingrained in his memory. His lifelong dream had been to find this great ship, and for thirteen years his quest for her had dominated his life. Now, finally, his quest was over.

Why do some people seem to find fulfillment, joy, and peace within their everyday lives while others feel they're trapped in the mediocre? What really makes the difference? *A dream that will not die and the unrelenting perseverance it takes to reach that dream—without giving up.* Many people have known such tenacity.

• Margaret Thatcher lived over her father's grocery store until she was twenty-one years old. But her dream gave her the perseverance to work until she achieved her goals, and today, as prime minister of Great Britain, she serves as the leader of one of the world's greatest nations.

• Many friends told Renoir to give up painting because he had no talent. In his later life, Renoir suffered from advanced rheumatism, particularly in his hands. When his friend Henri Matisse stopped by to see the aging painter, he noticed that every brush stroke caused Renoir extreme pain.

When Matisse asked Renoir why he continued to torture himself, he replied, "The pain passes. But the pleasure, the creation of beauty, remains."

• Jeff Steinberg was born with multiple birth defects, including no arms and stunted crippled legs. He spent the first two years of his life in a welfare shelter and later moved into a Shriner's Hospital for Crippled Children. He literally fought for his life in the hospital where he underwent numerous surgeries and learned to walk in braces and feed himself with a hook at the end of an artificial arm.

I heard Jeff speak before an audience of three thousand people. Pat Boone introduced him as "the Rocky of the Handicapped." Standing four feet six inches, Jeff held the microphone in his hook as he told humorous anecdotes, sang songs, and finally related his personal story. The audience, visibly moved and inspired, hung on his every word, responding to his warm, outgoing personality. I listened in awe that day as Jeff spoke the words that proved him a true champion: "I am God's unique design. I am proof that there is no limit to what a person can become, no matter what he or she may look like."

Shakespeare said it best: "Our doubts are traitors, and make us lose the good we oft might win, *by fearing to attempt.*" You must not be afraid of what God allows to happen to you. By giving up or becoming angry because of a difficult set of circumstances, you're saying in effect, "God, I reject Your plan for my life." You must hold onto your dreams and trust God to bring you through the tough times so you may achieve them. You must strive to become all you ever dreamed of becoming by turning your adversity to your advantage. And during your quest you must always remember that . . .

- No mountain is too high to keep you from climbing it.
- No obstacle is too awesome to keep you from overcoming it.
- No goal is too great to keep you from reaching it.
- No problem is too difficult to keep you from solving it.
- No adversary is too powerful to keep you from conquering it.
- No burden is too heavy to keep you from bearing it.
- No aspiration is too noble to keep you from attaining it. . . . as long as you have a dream.

We have dreams in our hearts not to taunt us, but because we're capable of achieving them. The fact that there is something in life we want is proof we're able to obtain it—if only we don't give up. God has a plan for each of us and most of the time it includes hard work on our part. Life is full of peaks and valleys. But the exciting thing is that the valleys are placed there for a reason—to make us stronger, to give us rest, to make us aware of our dependency on God. The secret is to look to the mountain and not give up. *It's always too soon to quit!*

2

Failure Is
Never Final

Mickey Mantle experienced 1,710 strikeouts and 1,734 walks during his career with the New York Yankees. That's 3,444 times that he came to bat without hitting the ball. If a man playing regularly gets around 500 at-bats per season, then Mantle played seven years without ever hitting the ball!

But what did Mickey Mantle do with his "failure." He had thousands of unproductive times at bat and other difficulties to face and overcome. Yet he became one of the most respected batting champions baseball has ever known. A person can always get up and try again. Mickey Mantle did.

No one, rich or poor, young or old, is immune to trouble. Everyone faces obstacles and disappointments. These things are a very real part of life, a part of the growing and learning process. But, why do some people overcome tragedies while others don't? Adversity causes some people to break down and others to break records. Some are simply more adept at learning from their difficulties and turning them to their advantage. It's not *what* happens to us in life that matters, but rather how we *react* to what happens.

We don't fail in life because we don't get any breaks or

because we aren't in the right place at the right time or because we've only experienced tough times. We fail from lack of the right action and lack of the right attitude. We fail because we accept defeat and give up too soon. The second truth you need to remember is *failure is never final*. We can make it through the tough times if we lean on God and refuse to accept defeat.

Following are some of the major reasons I believe people give up and quit too soon and, as a result, end up feeling like failures for the rest of their lives.

How to Fail

1. Don't Want a Goal Badly Enough. A young man approached me after a speech I had just given for his company.

"All those things you just said may sound good on the surface," he said. "But, they just won't work for me."

"Why not?" I asked.

"Well, all my life I've always wanted to be a lawyer. But, I married during college, and then our children came along. I had to go to work to support my young family as soon as I graduated, so I never got to go to law school."

"Why don't you go back now?"

"That's impossible!" he exclaimed. "I'm forty years old. I'd have to go to school part time at night, and it would take me at least five years to finish. Why, I'd be forty-five years old before I could get my law degree. I just couldn't do it. It's just too late."

"How old will you be in five years if you *don't* get your law degree?" I asked him.[1]

You see, he didn't want the law degree badly enough to go out and do something about it. In order to get the "breaks" in life, and in order to have the determination not to give up, a person must want a dream or a goal enough to make a decision to do something about it and then act upon that decision. Success doesn't just fall into your lap.

2. Accept Defeat and Place the Blame on Others.

After reviewing his teenage son's report card, an irate father exclaimed, "Five *F*s? How could you make five *F*s? This is the worst report card you've ever had!"

"What do you think it is, Dad," the boy asked, "heredity or environment?"

The second reason people give up and fail to grow or learn from life's experiences is that they have accepted defeat and placed the blame for that defeat on something or someone else. You're never a failure until you begin to shift the blame for your mistakes to circumstances or to others.

Practically every president who ever served blamed bad economic conditions, inflation, foreign unrest, unemployment, and so on on the previous administration. Workers blame colleagues when they don't get a promotion or can't get their jobs done. If people aren't blaming their peers, they're blaming their leaders for holding them back. If it isn't their leaders' fault, then it certainly must be that of a spouse. The wife nags too much, or the husband isn't a good provider and doesn't give enough support. If it isn't the fault of a spouse, then God must be punishing them.

I once made eleven speeches in one week. Each time that week, without fail, someone would rush up to me after the speech, shake my hand, and say, "I'm a self-made man" or "I'm a self-made woman." Not once did anyone tell me, "I'm a self-made failure." How quickly we take credit for our successes, but shift the blame for our failures to someone else. The people who overcome in life will continue to persevere during the tough times as well as during the good times. Failure is never final except for those who give up and refuse to accept responsibility for their own mistakes.

3. Anticipate Failure.

Babies are born with only two fears: the fear of falling and the fear of loud noises. All other fears must be *learned*. Fear is the most destructive force in the world. Fear cripples motivation. Fear destroys enthusiasm. Fear will eventually rob you of love. Fear destroys all desire, all hope, all ambition, and promotes worry, doubt, feelings of inadequacy, insecurity, and failure.

Called to give a paper before a group of learned psychologists, Dr. Will James, the father of American psychology, said, "Your belief at the beginning of any project determines its outcome." A major reason businesses fail, marriages break up, students do poorly in school, careers go sour, is fear—an attitude that *expects to fail*. Dr. James was the first to identify this as the Law of Self-Fulfilling Prophecy: *"Be careful of what you expect, because you're probably going to get it!"* History has proven out his theory. Winners *expect* to win just as losers *expect* to lose. This anticipation of failure is the major reason why some people give up and quit after a disappointing setback.

We were all created to do something meaningful and useful with our lives. The man or woman who thinks there is no chance for success destroys any such chance for accomplishment simply by acknowledging defeat before it ever occurs. Charles Darwin said, "The person who won't look up must look down." You can't go into any situation with a negative pessimistic attitude expecting to fail because that's the certain path to failure.

It's easy for us to expect failure because so much of what we hear each day is negative. There will always be those prophets of doom who say, "It can't be done." Some of them may be family members, some may be co-workers, and some are the so-called experts who have great influence. But many experts have been proven wrong in the past and many will be proven wrong in the future. What would have been our fate if some of the farsighted scientists and other innovative people who preceded us had allowed themselves to become tools of the skeptics and pessimists of their time?

• In the late 1800s a major university invited Bishop Wright to come and speak to its students. His topic: "The End of the World." Bishop Wright believed that the world would soon come to an end because all of the great inventions had already been invented. He believed that man had reached the ultimate in intellectual accomplishment, therefore nothing more could ever be achieved. He felt that if there was no more room for achievement, then God's purpose for man must certainly be finished.

One young professor in the audience that day incurred Bishop Wright's wrath by suggesting that man was yet to fly.

"If God had wanted man to fly," Bishop Wright thundered, "He would have given him wings!"

We are thankful today that Bishop Wright's two sons, Orville and Wilbur, didn't listen to their father's near-sighted ideas.

• In June 1833 the *Atlantic Journal* reported that too much violence and too many crimes were occurring in the world. The incessant strain of daily living made it impossible for people to keep pace. It went on to report that science poured its discoveries on people so quickly that they staggered beneath them in hopeless bewilderment. It said the political world was changing so rapidly that people became out of breath just trying to keep up with who's in and who's out. Human nature just couldn't endure much more.

• A few years later in November of 1857 the *Boston Globe* carried the following headline: **"Energy Crisis Looms! World to Go Dark! Whale Blubber Scarce!"**

Somehow we've managed to survive the scarcity of whale blubber and even more modern energy crises and progress beyond the prophecies of the "experts" of gloom and doom who saw a problem but couldn't see a solution. There are other historical events as well that may not have been quite the same had the people associated with them listened to their pessimistic critics:

• With the invention of the locomotive came the solemn warning that anyone who traveled at the breakneck speed of thirty miles per hour would probably suffocate. Claims were made that such speeds were extremely dangerous

and life-threatening. Therefore, the locomotive should be destroyed.

• A parliamentary committee was appointed in England to investigate Thomas Edison's revolutionary new electric light. After much deliberation, the committee concluded that the "light" was unworthy of the attention of practical scientific men who had much more important things to do.

• In the early 1900s, after Bishop Wright's famous speech, eminent scientists "proved" that the Wright brothers would never fly.

• Space flight seemed even more improbable. One astronomer as late as the 1950s made this classic remark: "Space travel is utter bilge!" I wonder what he thought when, only ten short years later, a young energetic president by the name of John Kennedy set his sights on the moon with an expectation for success beyond anything the space scientists had ever imagined.

In order to be successful, people must not anticipate failure with fear. Instead, they must learn from their past mistakes and failures and turn them into something positive in their lives. Thomas J. Watson, Jr., former president and chairman of the board of IBM, knew this well. He once told his employees that they must double their "failure rate." He knew that great ideas often come after great crises and that people learn from their mistakes. He wanted his people to learn how to grow *through* the tough times and turn them into something positive and fruitful.

Long before Alexander Graham Bell invented the telephone, a German schoolmaster named Wilhelm Reiss constructed a primitive telephonelike device through which he could transmit the sounds of whistling and humming. However, his gadget couldn't transmit speech— something was lacking. But Mr. Reiss, unable to find out what that something was right away, put the instrument aside and gave up.

Later, while working on his own version of the telephone, Alexander Graham Bell moved the screw that controlled the electrodes *a mere one-thousandth of an inch,* allowing the electrodes to touch. As a result, his telephone was able to transmit speech from one instrument to another. Bell's patient perseverance and *a fraction of an inch made all the difference between failure and success.*

That essential difference between success and failure in a person's life is determined by how he or she responds to circumstances and learns from them. True success depends more on your attitude than on your mental ability, more on your willingness to learn from your mistakes than on a diploma of any kind. The person who learns from failure and turns adversity into opportunity is the person who will grow and rise to the top in whatever he or she takes on in life.

4. *Don't Get Along Well With Others.* From owners of small "mom and pop" businesses, to managers and executives in larger companies, to presidents of companies, to leaders of nations, history has shown that the most successful people in any area of life have been good communicators. They know how to get along well with others.

According to court records, there are eight major reasons given for divorce. One of those eight reasons is lack of communication in the marriage. After four years of study and three separate surveys, the Princeton Opinion Research Poll revealed that the average husband and wife spend only *sixty seconds per day* talking with each other. No wonder there are so many divorces! Many marital problems could be avoided if husbands and wives would just talk openly and honestly.

The same Princeton poll also revealed that the average mother and/or father spends less than *twenty-nine minutes per week* in one-on-one communication with each child. And nine of those minutes are spent in disciplinary action. That leaves twenty minutes per week—*only three minutes per day*—spent in open, positive communication with the very people whose moral and social development critically depend upon their parents' leadership and guidance.

In a different survey 100,000 teenagers across the nation were asked what they wanted most from their parents. Four of the ten responses were: (1) answer our questions, (2) don't quarrel with us, (3) never lie to us, and (4) praise our good points. In light of the Princeton poll, it's not surprising that 40 percent of the teenagers' responses dealt with communication and personal interaction. Teenagers are crying out for their parents to talk to them. Over five thousand teens commit suicide each year. Are we really so busy that we don't have time for the very people who mean the most to us?

It's not so much different in the business world. A number of years ago one of America's largest companies ran an advertising campaign with the slogan "We Listen." The company adopted that slogan because a survey they conducted revealed that the number one complaint employees had was that their respective managers or supervisors never listened to them. Expecting employees to complain most about money, the company executives were shocked to learn that people were more concerned with communication.

Studies show that 71 percent of the leadership in the eighties and nineties will depend upon good communication skills. Seventy-five percent of a person's income depends upon his or her ability to communicate with others. People who don't practice good communicating skills often experience loss of jobs and even failed businesses. Knowing how to get along well with other people is essential for success in a job, career, social setting, or homelife.

5. *Depend Solely Upon Your Own Strengths and Resources.* Never is a person more alone as when he decides that he can "make it on his own." This is the person who says, "I'm self-made," or, "Look at what *I've* done with my life." Anyone can achieve material success, and many have. But that kind of success is only temporary. By definition, a person will never achieve permanent and everlasting success until he or she pursues a permanent and everlasting goal. Since all of us will someday pass away, no achievement we obtain on earth can be considered permanent. But we *can* establish a relationship with our Creator that will outlast anything we may accomplish in this life. The sooner this is done, the more time we will have to draw on that relationship for guidance, comfort, and strength.

During the National Football League players' strike in the fall of 1987, many of the players sought other things to keep them busy. Consequently, they frequently appeared on television talk shows, at charity benefits, and the like. During that time Gordon Banks of the Dallas Cowboys appeared on a Christian talk show where he was interviewed about his faith.

"I was a winner before I came to the NFL," he said. "And I'll be a winner after I leave, because I'll always have Jesus Christ with me."

Gordon Banks is definitely a success in this life. All the awards and achievements he has gained and will gain in the future are wonderful and, as far as I know, well deserved. He worked very hard for them. But he will lose most of that success and achievement when he dies. Gordon knows these honors are not permanent. He also knows what *is* permanent. One facet of his success—his relationship with his God—will never be erased.

Practically every success story I've ever heard or read has taken years and years of painstaking toil, sweat, tears, and hard labor—often in the face of voices of gloom and doom—before a person finally achieved "overnight success." Every great achievement worth having has come from a steady progression of small achievements. This is true throughout life. You eat a meal one bite at a time. You read a book one page at a time. You walk a mile one step at a time. You go through school one course at a time. You build up a savings account one dollar at a time. And our military leaders testify that big wars are won one battle at a time.

If you want to make it through the tough times and achieve success, you must stop looking around in envy at what others have done and focus on God and on yourself and on what the two of you can do *together* to make your dreams come true. Steve Allen, Debbie Reynolds, Mickey Mantle, Alexander Graham Bell, Calvin Peete, Joe Carcione, and Dr. Robert Ballard didn't feel sorry for themselves and give up. They did something about their plights in life—one small step at a time. Success is a direct result of action. Everything worth having is worth working for. Nothing in life is free. God gave the birds food, but He didn't throw it into their nests for them! They have to go out and work for it.

Success has nothing whatsoever to do with getting chance "breaks" in life. Success is a result of conscious decisions that a person makes about his or her life. And I believe that there are three major decisions a person must make—whether consciously or subconsciously—before he or she can accomplish great things:

Decide what you want. I will always believe that we have dreams for a reason and that reason isn't to be teased by our dreams. The fact that we dream is proof to me that we can achieve those dreams if we're willing to "pay the price" (work) to get them.

While in California in the summer of 1984, I heard about a young man who had been a sky diver until, on his nineteenth jump, his parachute failed to open fully. His emergency chute wrapped itself around the partially collapsed main chute, and he slammed into a dry lake bed at sixty miles per hour. Doctors thought this broken remnant of a man would never leave the hospital bed. When they told him this, he sank into a deep, black despair.

While in the hospital, the sky diver was frequently visited by another patient, a man whose spinal cord had been severed in a tragic automobile accident. Now a quadraplegic, this man would never walk nor lift a finger again. In spite of his condition, the young sky diver's visitor was always cheerful.

"I certainly wouldn't recommend my situation to anyone," he would say. "*And yet* I can read. I can listen to beautiful music. And I can talk to people."

"And yet." These words gave such hope to the sky diver that he came through his ordeal with a determination not to give up and quit. He focused not on what he had lost, but on what he could do with what he had left, on what he could gain by not giving up. He knew what he wanted and he concentrated on that with a positive attitude and an expectation of success. Today, to the amazement of his doctors, he walks without even a trace of a limp. Decide exactly what you want in life and go after it.

Decide you deserve success. If you feel you don't deserve success, perhaps you're suffering from poor self-esteem. In that case, you need to find a good book on how to build a positive self-image.[2] Without good self-esteem, your subconscious mind will fight you all your life and ensure that you fail.

If you honestly believe that you have a right to be successful, to achieve your dreams and overcome the obstacles in your path, then your chances of actually doing so will improve. Because people usually get what they expect. This goes back to the Law of Self-Fulfilling Prophecy again. If you *expect* to achieve, you will work to do the necessary things to overcome your obstacles and reach your goals. If you *expect* to fail, you will think, *What's the use? Why even try?* And you will fail.

A drunken derelict lay in a heap in the infamous New York City neighborhood known as the Bowery—a place of filth, drugs, cheap booze, loneliness, and disease. A compassionate passerby found him bruised, bleeding, and semiconscious. He took him to Bellevue Hospital where the derelict was admitted as a "John Doe." He languished in Bellevue for three long and lonely days until he died . . . still unknown.

A friend seeking him out was directed to the local morgue where he found the derelict, lying among dozens of other corpses with tags hanging from their still toes. The friend gathered up the personal effects—a dirty tattered coat with thirty-eight cents in one pocket and a scrap of paper in the other. Scrawled across the dirty scrap of paper were five words: *Dear friends and gentle hearts.*

Why would a forgotten drunk carry around such beautiful poetic words? Maybe he believed he still had it in him. Maybe deep within his being he still felt he deserved something better. But maybe that belief wasn't quite strong enough to give him the confidence and hope he needed to keep going without giving up his dream.

The derelict with the body of a bum had a heart and mind of a genius. For once upon a time, long before his tragic death at the young age of thirty-eight, Stephen Foster had written songs that had literally made the whole world sing. The South had danced to the tunes of "Camptown Races," "Oh! Susanna," "Jeannie With the Light Brown Hair," "Beautiful Dreamer," "My Old Kentucky Home," "Old Folks at Home," and two hundred more that have become deeply rooted in our rich southern American folk heritage.

One can only speculate that if young Stephen Foster had felt he really deserved something better, he would have worked harder at becoming all he wanted to become. He wouldn't have given up and turned to drink and destitution. Decide that you deserve your dreams.

Decide the price you're willing to pay for your dreams. A friend of mine once told me he'd give a thousand dollars to be a millionaire. Folks, that's not the price! It costs to give up and quit. Did you know that? It also costs to be a success. It only costs nothing to be mediocre. It may be enjoyable and comfortable to be mediocre, but looking back at the results can be very painful. You must decide if the end result is worth what it costs you to get there.

While attending tiny Campbell College in North Carolina, twenty-three-year-old Orville Peterson worked desperately to win a place on the United States track team. After the first day of the decathlon tryouts, Peterson held a solid eighth place in a field of fifty entrants. However, on the second day during the first event, the 110-meter hurdles, disaster paid a visit. Orville Peterson pulled muscles and ligaments in his left thigh that rendered him virtually immobile.

No one imagined that he could continue with the kind of

excruciating pain he must have been enduring. But, they were wrong because Orville Peterson had come to compete. He first refused to see even a trainer for fear he'd be forced to withdraw from the competition. So Orville continued in the next event, the discus throw. While experiencing agonizing pain in his leg, he managed to throw the heavy discus 137 feet, 5 inches. After accomplishing this seemingly impossible feat, he then managed to pole vault an amazing 12 feet, 5 inches as well as throw the javelin 206 feet, 9 inches. But these performances, while good under such circumstances, caused him to drop to fourteenth in the standings. Only one event remained on the second day of competition—the grueling 1,500 meters—four laps of pure hell for even the most fit and healthy athletes.

The crack of the start gun broke the heavy silence as spectators watched in eager anticipation, wondering how this brave young man could even make it around the first lap. The winner crossed the finish line in just under five minutes with the rest of the field close behind him. The track was then empty except for one lone runner.

Orville Peterson, his left thigh heavily wrapped, had promised himself that he'd complete the decathlon competition—even if he didn't win a place on the American team. In spite of his debilitating injury, he was willing to pay the price to achieve his dream. To do this, Orville had to finish the 1,500 meters, even if it meant he would have to limp all the way . . . and limp he did.

As the crowd began to cheer Peterson on, his fellow competitors lined the sides of the track and shouted their support. Then the beautiful strains of the theme from *Chariots of Fire* poured out of the public address loud speakers, filling the stadium with inspiring music. To Orville, this was bigger and better and meant more than becoming another Carl Lewis, Bruce Jenner, or Mary Decker. It was bigger than signing endorsement contracts for sports equipment or athletic clothing, or even bigger than making public appearances.

As Orville entered the home stretch of his final lap of that painful race and headed for the finish line, the PA

announcer quietly read this ancient Greek say
listening crowd:

> Never ask for victory, ask only for courag
> you endure the struggle, you bring honor to
> but most importantly, you bring honor to us

Peterson's time in the 1,500 meters that
9:44:80. He earned no points for his effort and
thirty-second place in the final standings. But
were there will testify that Orville Peterso
biggest winner of all because he endured the st
he was willing to pay the price and remain true

Orville Peterson's efforts will forever reflec
that how we react to life's circumstances dete
legacy we shall leave. Success is dependent
willingness to pay the price—a price that doesr
you compromise your beliefs and convictions
cess, but one which will enable you to striv
dreams and be proud of what you've done.

Successful people don't give up and quit whe
gets rough. They don't look at others and wis
the same "breaks." Successful people get bac
they fall and try again. They *make their own br*
People who achieve, in spite of the tough times
want something badly enough to (2) *persevere* t
tough times and (3) *pay the price* in order to
They face up to their responsibilities and worl
their circumstances for the better. Through al
(4) maintain a *positive attitude that expects to*
addition, they learn how to (5) *get along* with ot
And they (6) *surrender to a power beyond the*
guidance, strength, and support.

I have found these to be the six key charac
the successful people I've met over the years, a
like to share them with you throughout Part 2 o
I would like to show you why failure is nev
sharing ways in which you can make your own
life and by showing you that *it's always too so*

Part Two

Six Steps
to
Getting the
"Breaks" in Life

3

Burning Desire to Succeed

O
ne hot summer day in 1984, the inhabitants of a small New Mexico town lined the roadside as they awaited the arrival of a lone figure on the horizon. A strong young runner, beating a steady rhythm on the pavement as he approached his destination, proudly held a flaming torch high above his head with his right hand. His leg of the run was almost over. He would soon pass the torch to the next bearer who anxiously awaited his arrival. Nine-year-old Amy stood in the crowd and watched as the runner swiftly approached. Severely crippled and bent nearly double, Amy had dreamed of carrying the Olympic torch on one leg of its long journey from Athens, Greece, to Los Angeles, California.

When Amy took the heavy torch from the runner, she had to hold it with both hands. Amy didn't possess the strength and agility of her predecessor, but she bravely took first one halting step and then another. The motorcycle policeman who was to escort the torchbearer through town impatiently gunned his engine. The little girl took another halting step. The policeman grew even more impatient and finally moved ahead.

As the crowd gave her words of encouragement, Amy raised her head, revealing a beautiful face with twinkling eyes and a broad smile. Everyone knew she couldn't carry the torch for a kilometer as those who had gone before her, but the determination in her eyes told them she would certainly try.

This little girl possessed a deep burning desire to do this one thing in life. She wanted this more than anything in the world. So Amy and her mother had raised the necessary fee of three thousand dollars by holding bake sales and garage sales in their front yard. Amy trained for a year with a ten-pound hammer so her fragile arms could support the torch for a full kilometer. During training, she was not once able to complete the distance. But she never once gave up trying.

The crowd grew to fifteen- and twenty-deep on both sides of the road. They held balloons, flags, and banners that read, "Run, Amy, Run." They cheered and shouted words of encouragement. The local high school band played patriotic songs. And all the while, Amy was settling into a steady rhythm—much slower than that of a seasoned runner, but a rhythm just the same. Everyone present that day felt something special. They knew this wasn't an ordinary day or an ordinary little girl. Amy's determination and desire moved hearts. Cameramen put down their cameras for a moment to reach for handkerchiefs and wipe away tears. Even the impatient policeman, who had stopped his motorcycle several yards ahead of Amy, brushed away a tear as he watched her display such great courage.

Many inspiring stories emerged from the 1984 Olympics. But the greatest story didn't occur in Los Angeles. The greatest story played out in the streets of a small New Mexico town. Amy completed the kilometer run that day—for the first time since she had started training one year earlier. This little athlete climbed her Mount Everest. She won her gold medal. She accomplished what no one thought she could.

Little Amy possesses what I believe to be the first characteristic of successful people who overcome defeat to accomplish their dreams and turn setbacks into success: a *burning desire to succeed*. She wanted her dream badly enough to do something about it. The look of triumph on her pretty little face at the end of the kilometer run told the world just how much she wanted it. Amy achieved success at a very early age because she knew that, regardless of the size of the dream before her, *it's always too soon to quit!*

History has proved that every great person was an unknown until he or she became consumed with a dream and a desire that burned within compelling him or her to do whatever was necessary to achieve those dreams.

• Charles Schwab was a stake driver who had a burning desire within that drove him to eventually become the master of the steel industry.

• John Rockefeller was a bookkeeper making twenty-five dollars a month who followed a burning desire within and ultimately became master of an oil empire.

• I doubt that many people know why the Crimean War was fought, not to mention any of the generals who fought in it. But during that war, one compassionate young lady became so committed to those suffering in agony from their wounds that she walked among the wounded to tend them and ease their pain. Today the nursing world rings with the name of Florence Nightingale whose burning desire to help others led to the establishment of the nursing profession.

• Although crippled with arthritis, author Clarence Day had such a desire to create that he taped a pencil to his hand and continued to write. In the days before electric typewriters, personal computers, and dictation equipment, Day painfully wrote out the scenes of "Life With Father" which brought laughter to millions across the radio waves of America.

• What else, other than a burning desire, explains the life of John Bunyan? While confined to prison in Bedford Jail, and while listening to his young daughter pleading with him to give up and admit there was no God, John Bunyan refused to be defeated and wrote *Pilgrim's Progress,* second only to the Bible in the inspiration it has given to millions of people.

• A high school senior in Oklahoma walked across the stage to receive his high school diploma. The principal singled him out and asked him to tell the audience what he wanted to do with his life.

Johnny turned and told the crowd, "I'm going to be the greatest catcher in baseball."

The audience responded with peals of laughter. But years later when Johnny Bench became the number one catcher in all of baseball, his critics stopped laughing. He had a burning desire to succeed.

• In 1968 a fifteen-year-old boasted that he'd win seven gold medals at the Mexico City Olympics. People laughed at him, too. They laughed even louder when, at the end of the Olympic games, he had won only two gold medals.

That young man spent the next four years in intensive training—four hours a day, seven days a week. At the next Olympic games Mark Spitz set seven world records in seven different swimming events and won his seven gold medals. His burning desire to succeed gave him the ability to "pay the price" to accomplish his dream. And his critics laughed no more.

• Paralyzed from the neck down since age six, Paul Alexander has spent most of his life in an iron lung. Paul miraculously survived the polio epidemic that gripped Dallas, Texas, during the 1950s.

Wanting desperately to live moments of his life outside the iron monstrosity, Paul taught himself to "gulp" air when he was around age ten. He partially weaned himself from the lung so he could steal moments and, finally, hours of freedom from it. He can now survive outside the lung for up to twenty-four hours at a time. Paul also taught himself to write with his mouth so he could complete his dream of going to college and law school—a dream that took him fifteen years to accomplish.

At age forty, Paul was admitted to the bar in Austin, Texas, in May 1986. His mother says that although he has a body that won't go, Paul has a brain and a personality that won't stop. His burning desire to succeed has enabled him to accomplish the seemingly impossible. Who could ask for more?

• Born prematurely into a poverty-stricken inner-city family, Laura Jones exemplifies a burning desire to succeed. An over-supply of oxygen in her incubator after birth left Laura legally blind. Her protective mother thought Laura would be hurt in a public school and didn't want to send her away to a special school either. So Laura didn't begin first grade until she was ten years old. Timid and shy and unable to see the chalkboard and the small print in her books, Laura began her education at a great disadvantage. But that education was to be the key to something bigger and better than Laura had ever imagined.

Moved into a class for students needing special education when she was in the second grade, Laura soon met the teacher who would become her mentor as well as her cheerleader. With her new teacher's encouragement, Laura developed an insatiable thirst for education and she breezed through the next four years of elementary school.

Laura discovered music in elementary school and she began playing the cornet in hopes that she could someday march with the high school band. When she reached high school, her band director placed her with the tubas, a section that marched in the back row and wasn't as visible as the brass line in front. Undaunted by this action, Laura's desire for her rightful place in the band enabled her to work harder than she had ever worked before. By her junior year, she had earned not only a solo position, but also a place with the rest of the cornets in the front row where she belonged.

Laura Jones had two dreams. Her first dream was to get a college education—something no one in her family of nine brothers and sisters had ever accomplished. Fueled from childhood, Laura's thirst for education could not be quenched and she struggled to catch up on what she'd missed by starting school four years later than her peers. She graduated from high school nineteenth in her class and received scholarships from local civic and state organizations. Now her first dream could be viewed as a reality.

Laura's second dream was to march with her state university's marching band. She thought this would be easy since she had marched in high school. But she soon learned that her high school classmates had helped her more than she realized by telling her when she was out of line or out of step. When she failed to qualify for the marching band, she didn't let that little disappointment defeat her. She simply set a new goal. Today, as a sophomore, Laura plays her cornet in her university's basketball band which keeps the spirits high at the men's home games. She feels her second dream has come true.

Laura has set a new goal to become a vision teacher and help children like herself—children who need a friend as she did when she was a child. If her past accomplishments are an example, I'm sure that she won't have any trouble achieving her goal because Laura Jones never let a little failure here and there defeat her. She didn't let a disability get in the way of achieving her dreams. The desire that burned within her urged her to work to become all that she ever wanted to become—and more than others thought she could become.

Stories like Laura's prove to me that each of us has a choice in life. When we're faced with difficulties and adversity, we can either give up or keep on. Napoleon Hill said that every achievement in mankind, no matter what its nature or purpose, must begin with an intense *burning desire for success*. That's the secret—not power, not fate, not prestige, not position, not wealth, not chance. A person must *want* to succeed. A person must make the decision to keep going through the tough times. The tragic lives are those of people who don't desire anything badly enough to have faith that the difficulties can be used to make us stronger. The tragic lives are those of people who aren't willing to work for success, who make the choice to give up and quit.

You Have to Want Success

A young boy orphaned at age three was taken into the home of John Allan who became his foster father, although he never legally adopted him. When Mrs. Allan died a few years later and John remarried, the relations between Mr. Allan and his young foster child became severely strained and finally severed.

This young man's life was dominated by failure. He attended a classical academy, several colleges, and enlisted for a brief period in the army. He was expelled from the University of Virginia for gambling debts he was unable to pay as well as from West Point for infractions of numerous rules.

In spite of his conduct, this man possessed enormous literary talent. By age eighteen he had already published two collections of poetry. By twenty-eight, he had published poems and short stories in literary magazines throughout the Northeast—none of which was given the slightest critical or popular acclaim. His many detractors scorned and laughed at his work.

In 1836, at age twenty-seven, he married his thirteen-year-old cousin, Virginia Clemm. His burden of constant debt and a constant drinking habit, however, prevented him from adequately caring for his family. When Virginia died eleven years later of tuberculosis, he wrote his next poem "Annabell Lee" to her.

In 1845 he moved to New York to work on the *Evening Mirror* which first published his poem "The Raven." This poem finally established his national reputation, although by then he had begun to receive adequate recognition for his other work. Within one year he became co-editor and owner of his own publication, the *Broadway Journal,* which promptly collapsed the same year.

His drinking increased over the years and some scholars believe he used narcotics. A series of drinking bouts left him exhausted, and in October 1849 he was found seriously ill by friends who took him to a nearby hospital. He died several days later at age forty.

Ironically it wasn't until after his death that Edgar Allan Poe received the acclaim due him for his literary genius. Today, more books have been written about him than about any other American author. He is recognized and respected as a poet and author of short stories, books of criticism, and newspaper reviews. At a Christmas literary auction in New York City in 1976, *Tamerlane and Other Poems*—his first book which was totally ignored when he wrote it—brought a record price of $123,000, the highest price paid for any published literary work.

Poe had experienced rejection since early childhood. He had lost both his natural and foster parents. Perhaps this partly explains his conduct which resulted in many of his troubles as an adult, although ultimate responsibility for his behavior lies with him. Although Poe possessed an enormous talent, he didn't have enough desire to persevere through the tough times. A known alcoholic and drug addict, he was unwilling to obey God. And he was unwilling to pay the price necessary for a rewarding success in his chosen career. He had failed to learn from his experiences and grow through the tough times. His posthumous success came too late for Poe who died believing himself to be a miserable failure.

We all go through tough times, and we all fail at one time or another. I've carried the following quote in my wallet for years. These words by an unknown author have helped me through many times of testing. Perhaps they'll help you as well.

Failing doesn't mean I'm a failure; it just means I haven't yet succeeded.

Failing doesn't mean I've accomplished nothing; it just means I've learned something.

Failing doesn't mean I've been a fool; it just means I had enough faith to experiment.

Failing doesn't mean I've been disgraced; it just means I dared to try.

Failing doesn't mean I don't have what it takes; it just means I must do things differently next time.

Failing doesn't mean I'm inferior; it just means I'm not perfect.

Failing doesn't mean I've wasted my time; it just means I have a reason to start over.

Failing doesn't mean I should give up; it just means I must try harder.

Failing doesn't mean I'll never make it; it just means I
need more patience.

Failing doesn't mean I'm wrong; it just means I must find
a better way.

Failing doesn't mean God has abandoned me; it just means
I must obediently seek His will.

On September 17, 1935, Violet Oggs gave birth at home
to a son suffering from severe brain damage. The doctors at
the hospital to which he was taken said he would not live
more than a few hours. And if he did live he would never
walk, talk, or see. But the doctors didn't know what fervent
prayer could do. The faithful prayers of family and friends
pulled Allan C. Oggs through his first day of life and he
survived to face his life afflicted with cerebral palsy.

Allan's parents refused to allow him to use his disability
as an excuse for not doing whatever he wanted to do nor
would they allow him to ever feel sorry for himself.
Although his coordination, balance, and speech were affected, he tried what most any other child would try—from
riding a bicycle to playing touch football—many times
getting hurt in the process. *Can't* and *crippled* were words
not found in his vocabulary.

In his sophomore year in high school, Allan felt called to
preach. People from all over his community tried to
discourage him, pointing out that his physical limitations
would prevent him from becoming an effective minister.
But Allan Oggs wanted to preach. So the young teenager
asked God to give him a sign—if he was to be a preacher,
he would not only be invited as the guest speaker at the
next youth rally, but he would be asked to preach as well.
In addition, he wanted to preach an effective sermon.

You can guess the rest of the story! Not only was Allan
invited to the youth rally and asked to preach, but he was
able to preach for over an hour to a very receptive
audience. His calling had been confirmed. Allan went on
to attend the seminary where he met his future wife,
Gwen Vanderhoff. Together they would later have three
beautiful children.

Allan Oggs has been a preacher now for over thirty years. He has faced many peaks and valleys in his life. He overcame a physical handicap and went against all advice from doctors and friends to do that thing which he loved most. He did what others told him he couldn't. He has been able to make it through the valleys in his life and learn from the experience because he possesses a burning desire to succeed. He describes this desire as "the want-to."

"Everywhere I go," Allan says, "I am sharing the message of the 'want-to.' There is nothing I have accomplished that you can't accomplish also. . . .

"When they looked for somebody to try an artificial heart on, they weren't just looking for physical characteristics. They chose a man who was known to have the tenacity and will of a bulldog. When they cut him open and stuck a machine in his chest, he had to have more than muscle. He had to have grit. He had to be a fighter. Barney Clark had learned the secret of success. He knew the question is not whether you *can,* but whether you *want to.* If you want something badly enough, are willing to work for it, and will surrender the ultimate outcome to God, there is no limit to what you can achieve. You will be surprised and amazed at what you can do, if you really have the 'want-to.' "[1]

Allan Oggs overcame a physical disability that affected his muscular control and speech to become something that most everyone told him he couldn't—all because he had the desire in his heart to do something he believed in and cared about. Read all the books on success and you will find that after the mastery of the fundamentals, the remainder consists primarily of desire. You have to *want* something badly enough that you will be willing to pay the price and do whatever is necessary to accomplish it. Success is a direct result of *acting* on those desires in order to accomplish your dreams.

If there has been something in your life that you've wanted so badly you could taste it, then get up and go after it. Because that's the kind of burning desire it takes for a person to be really successful and then happy in that success. Maybe you can't quit your current job to pursue this dream. But there's always a way. Whether it's going back to school part-time, or whether it's allowing a beloved hobby to become a part-time avocation, the end result is worth the price if it's something you really and truly desire for your life.

Listen to your inner yearnings. If you have a deep, burning desire to be something different, to do something different with your life, then you have the great potential to make it! But whether or not you do is entirely up to you. God has given you the ability and the desire. Now you must take the necessary *action* to accomplish your dreams.

Thomas Edison once said, "Genius is 1 percent inspiration and 99 percent perspiration." Without the 99 percent effort on your part, you'll always remain simply a *potential* success. Regardless of the past or the present, you have the *potential* to become whatever you *want* to become. You even have the ability to enlist God's help and draw from His power to achieve your dreams. *It's always too soon to quit!*

4

Reviresco:
I Flourish
in Adversity

W hile reading a magazine on a flight to San Francisco, I came across a picture of a dead tree stump out of which grew a small green shoot. The picture was entitled *Reviresco*. I later learned that this is a Latin word meaning, "I flourish in adversity." The picture reminded me of another scene watched on television by millions of Americans in the fall of 1987.

In September of that year raging forest fires consumed over half a million acres of forest land and watershed in California and Oregon. More than twenty thousand firemen and national guardsmen battled for over a month to gain control of the fires. When it was over, officials walked through the massive devastation to survey the damage. There they found, rising above the smoking ashes and blackened tree stumps, literally thousands of seedling Ponderosa pines, miraculously untouched by the fires.

Sprouting from pine cones dropped from parent trees, these small seedlings had little chance of survival prior to the fires. Before, they had to compete with the adult trees for light from the sun and nutrition from the soil in an already crowded forest. But after the fires they could reach toward the sun and find new life not possible before. Flourishing within surrounding adversity, these small uns and bronze cannons, and target shooting. Yes, target shooting. He uses an electronic chirping bird for an audio target so he can find the direction of the target through sound.

As a result of his courage and his interest in and involvement with church and social organizations, Jim has received numerous awards and much recognition. He was named National Rehabilitant by the United States Department of Health and Human Services in 1970. He has received the Meritorious Service Citation from the President's Committee on Employment of the Handicapped, the United States Presidential Commendation for Exceptional Service, the Certificate of Distinguished Citizenship from the state of Maryland, and the Johns Hopkins Certificate of Achievement. In 1983 the city of Austin named Jim Handicapped Person of the Year. And in 1984 he was named Texas Disabled Employee. But, perhaps Jim's highest honor came in 1985 when, on May 2, United States Secretary of Labor William Brock presented him with the President's Trophy for the Handicapped American of the Year—an award presented by the President's Committee on Employment of the Handicapped.

Jim Caldwell's attitude can best be summed up in his own words. "Being handicapped," he says, "is just a state of mind . . . I, probably more than most, realize how the buffeting of life solidifies values. It has taken a good deal of hard experience to know at a visceral level that there is a power greater than ourselves who can, will, and does support us at anytime simply for the asking. I believe that with this help few things are impossible and that reliance upon God's guidance is the path to a happy and satisfying life."

Jim Caldwell's doctors told him he would never again function as a productive person in society. His determination, courage, and tenacity proved them wrong. He certainly knows the meaning of the word reviresco. He has flourished in adversity greater than most people will ever experience. He knows how to turn a crisis into an opportunity. He knows that God is there to help us just for the asking. And he knows it's always too soon to quit.

seedlings promised a bountiful forest for future generations. New life had sprung out of the ashes of death.

That's the story of success. The people who are able to come from the pitfalls in life and rise above them are the people who can flourish in the tough times. They have the unique ability to refuse to be defeated and somehow always manage to flourish in spite of the hand life has dealt them.

A study of the five hundred most successful men in America revealed that these men shared what I believe to be the second characteristic of successful people—an indispensable ingredient that seemed to run like a common thread throughout their lives—they *flourished in adversity*. They never gave up after failure. Instead, they actually made *plans* to overcome the odds they faced. Out of the ashes of their defeats blossomed the strength and success that history has honored and time rewarded. Anyone can quit. That's the easy way out. But the successful keep coming back and trying again and again and again.

Just a State of Mind

August 9, 1962, began like any other day for Jim Caldwell, a twenty-five-year-old navy veteran and engineer living in Annapolis, Maryland. For several weeks he had been working on his passion, the *Sabrina*—a wooden native Chesapeake sailboat with bronze fittings and canvas sails. That evening he planned to go down to her mooring and complete some last-minute touch-up work and painting so he and friends could go sailing the next day. But first, he planned to barbecue some chicken for dinner.

Jim entered his backyard to start a fire in his barbecue grill. He tried to light the grill once with some paper but it went out. Remembering that the fuel in the boat's stove could be used for lighting camp fires, he retrieved a gallon can of it and looked carefully to make sure there was no fire in the barbecue kettle. When he sprayed the fuel on the charcoal, flames raced up the stream of alcohol and into the can which immediately exploded. Over half of the flaming liquid sprayed over Jim, resulting in first- and second-degree burns over 70 percent of his body.

Jim was taken to a hospital where he was able to sit and walk, and for a time he appeared reasonably stable. But he soon began losing strength in his legs, became confused and disoriented, lost his vision, and lapsed into a coma that lasted nearly a month. At this point he was transferred to Johns Hopkins Hospital in Baltimore, where he finally awoke from his coma to learn that in addition to his severe burns, he was now permanently blind and paralyzed from the waist down.

Upon receiving this devastating news, Jim concerned himself not with his handicaps so much as with the matters of surviving in a new and different world: of coping with the very long and slow process of recovery, of learning to dress and feed himself, and of learning to adjust to his new life in darkness and in a wheelchair. After two years of treatment in the hospital, his doctors told him that he would always have to live in a protected environment, that he would need constant care, and that he had no chance of ever getting a meaningful job or living a normal life because he had "no rehabilitation potential." Jim reacted to this news by packing his bag. With the help of a friend he left the hospital and took an apartment—alone. Here he learned to care for himself and cope with living in the outside world.

A graduate in mechanical engineering, Jim now had to face the problem of finding a new way to make a living. In order to prove that he could put in an eight-hour day, he worked for a few months in an Easter Seals shelter workshop in Baltimore where he packed bags with small parts, stuffed envelopes, and sanded flower paintings from trash cans. When his supervisors told him he had potential and could advance to floor supervisor within five years, he politely thanked them and said he had other things in mind.

It was during this time that Jim's counse[...] about an experimental grant project at the U[...] Cincinnati—a project established to determi[...] blind people could operate computers. The [...] peaked his interest and together they put the [...] motion to enable Jim to become a computer pr[...] Jim obtained IBM programmed instruction m[...] the basic course material and hired a quadriple[...] for him. (An interesting footnote to this story is [...] reader ended up becoming a computer progr[...] well!) Jim had taken the first step toward a ne[...]

Once he mastered a new discipline, Jim's next [...] was to convince employers that he could be a p[...] and useful employee. He spent another year in [...] deavor, but his persistence paid off. After show[...] his abilities by converting their 1401 printer into [...] printer, Jim managed to convince the Chesa[...] Potomac Telephone Company of Baltimore that h[...] useful asset to their company. In October 1966, fo[...] after his accident, the telephone company hired h[...] computer programmer. Jim Caldwell had achieve[...] all the experts had said he could not—and he [...] through.

Plagued with flu brought on by the cold Ma[...] winters, Jim was easily persuaded by a friend from [...] that he might benefit from a warmer climate. In 1[...] moved to Austin where he enrolled at the Univer[...] Texas to pursue a doctorate in management scien[...] operations research. While at UT, he ran his own i[...] ment firm, maintained nearly a straight-A average (e[...] for two courses), and was elected to the Phi Kappa[...] National Honor Society. Eight years later in 197[...] earned his Ph.D. After graduation Jim joined IB[...] Austin as a systems analyst.

Jim Caldwell once told a reporter that if his life [...] any fuller, he couldn't stand it. Married since 1976, he [...] his wife, Sue, have three children. In addition to his w[...] he continues to pursue his favorite hobbies: woodwork[...] playing the bagpipes, operating a ham radio, collect[...]

What a marvelous example! Every human being has to decide again and again, and still again, whether to face fearsome difficulties or run away. You can't outrun fear or adversity—but you *can* face either head-on.

An old cowboy once told a story of how he had worked all his life on ranches where each year winter storms took heavy tolls among the cattle. Temperatures often dipped quickly below zero and freezing rains whipped across the prairies, driving flying ice cutting into the flesh. Howling, bitter winds piled swirling snow into enormous drifts so that any error in a person's step could send him plunging into a mountain of freezing white powder.

In this maelstrom of nature's violence most cattle would turn their backs to the icy blasts and slowly drift downwind until, intercepted by a boundary fence, they would huddle together against the snow-covered barrier. Standing motionless and helpless against nature's fury, the herd would slowly become covered by blowing snow and cattle would die by the scores.

But the Hereford breed reacted much differently. These cattle would instinctively head toward the windward end of the range where they would stand shoulder-to-shoulder with bowed heads, facing the storm's icy onslaught.

"You almost always found the Herefords alive and well," the old cowboy said. "I guess that's the greatest lesson I ever learned on the prairie—just to meet adversity head-on and face life's storms."[1]

We can't attempt to evade the things we're afraid of. We must face life head-on and try to find the good in each situation. We must learn to turn each crisis into an opportunity.

Most often carrying a negative connotation, the word *crisis* is defined by Webster's dictionary as an unstable or crucial time or state of affairs. It defines *opportunity,* a word that usually carries a positive connotation, as a favorable juncture of circumstances.

In the Chinese language, entire words and concepts are written with one symbol. Sometimes these symbols are combined to make a new meaning or word. The two individual Chinese characters used separately to mean *trouble* and *crisis* both carry negative connotations. However, when brought together and used as a pair, the two mean something entirely opposite: *opportunity*.

The same could be said of trials and obstacles in a person's life. A crisis that appears to one person as calamity may be viewed by another as an opportunity. Same problem, different perspective. You can look upon your "lot" in life with fear or with courage. It's all up to you.

Author, medical missionary, explorer, and discoverer of Victoria Falls, Dr. David Livingstone spent most of his adult life living in primitive conditions in Africa. Between 1857 and 1865 he led an exploration team on an expedition into eastern and central Africa which laid the foundation of Nyasaland. Although tiresome, fatiguing, and dangerous, Dr. Livingstone's work was to him a labor of love.

While exploring in Africa, Dr. Livingstone received a letter from some very well-meaning friends which read, "We would like to send other men to you. Have you found a good road into your area yet?"

Dr. Livingstone sent this message in reply, "If you have men who will only come if they know there is a good road, I don't want them. I want strong and courageous men who will come if there is no road at all."

An ancient proverb reminds us that "Courage consists not so much in avoiding danger as in conquering it." It is mastering our fears and getting on with the wonderful things life has to offer even when it appears there is no road at all on which to travel.

- Courage is *reviresco*. It takes courage to flourish in adversity and face life's disappointments head-on.
- Courage is the mastery over fear. It is not allowing fear to take over and control our lives. But rather, it is making plans for ways to overcome those fears.
- Courage is accepting the responsibilities that it would be more comfortable not to accept.
- Courage is persevering when life has dealt a seemingly losing hand. It is turning your crisis into an opportunity.

• Courage is performing the task that it would be easier
not to do. When nineteenth-century minister, orphanage
director, and author George Mueller was asked the secret
to his success, he answered, "As I look back on my life, I
see that I was constantly brought to a crossroads which
demanded a choice of which way I should go. I believe the
key to my success is that I seemed to have consistently
chosen the *least traveled path*." Courage is taking the
road least traveled.

To the courageous this "losing hand" (failure, fear,
rejection, disappointment, disability, etc.) simply fuels the
inner spirit to rise above it and respond. The interesting
truth in life is that our failures far outnumber our successes. So, how do we maintain the courage to "keep on
keeping on"? We can learn from the examples that have
been set by the courageous men and women who have
gone before—the men and women who have flourished in
adversity.

On the night of December 9, 1914, Edison Industries of
West Orange, New Jersey, burned to the ground. Thomas
Edison lost $2 million that evening as much of his life's
work went up in flames. He had only insured his "invention factory" for $238,000 because the building was
constructed of concrete, a material then thought to be
fireproof.

Fearing the worst, twenty-four-year-old Charles Edison
ran about frantically searching for his father. He finally
found him standing near the fire, his white hair blowing in
the cold December wind and his face ruddy from the glow
of the roaring flames.

"My heart ached for him," Charles said. "He was
sixty-seven years old—no longer a young man—and everything he'd worked for was going up in smoke."

When the elder Edison spotted his son coming toward
him, he shouted, "Charles, where's your mother?"

When the son answered that he didn't know, Mr. Edison
responded, "Well, find her and bring her here. She'll never
see anything like this again as long as she lives!"

The next morning as Edison walked through the charred remains of all his hopes and dreams he told his family, "There is a great value in disaster. It burns up all your mistakes. Thank God we can start anew."

Thomas Edison knew the meaning of *reviresco*. Three months after that devasting fire, Edison Industries presented the world with its first phonograph.

That's the story of a man who faced adversity head-on. He walked directly into the wind and faced the inevitable hazards of human existence with fortitude, courage, and faith. He knew that sixty-seven years meant nothing, and that the loss of a business meant nothing, because he could always rise above the ashes of his defeat and "start anew."[2]

• A young pilot crash-landed the first two times he soloed. The third time he flew alone, he flew head-on into another plane! He didn't let adversity stop him. He came back and tried again. Richard Byrd later became an outstanding pilot who would eventually make history by flying to the South Pole.

• A struggling young author wrote and tried to sell over forty books before his first was published. He never became discouraged or gave up trying. His perseverance paid off and Rod Serling later became a famous mystery writer and host of TV's "The Twilight Zone."

• Baseball player Pete Gray never won any home run titles and never led the field in batting. He was too slow to steal bases. And he only played part of one year in the major leagues. But Pete Gray is a baseball immortal whose name will go down in the annals of sports history. As a young man, Pete had an accident that left him with only one arm. But his courage and tenacity enabled him to achieve his lifelong dream of playing in the major leagues—even if it was only for a brief moment.

• On April 6, 1909, Matthew Henson, a member of Admiral Peary's expedition, stood on top of the world and planted the American flag in the freezing ice and snow of the North Pole. Henson displayed courage and perseverance because in an era of discrimination and second-class citizenry, the fact that he was black didn't stop him from pursuing his dream.

• Someone once asked Eleanor Roosevelt if her husband had not suffered from polio, would he still have become president of the United States. Mrs. Roosevelt replied, "Yes, but not the *same kind* of president." He had gained strength and courage from a defeat in his life that he probably otherwise would not have had.

What do you do when it seems as though there is no way out? How do you get yourself to realize that it's always too soon to quit? First, find a nice quiet place—away from the children, away from the television set, away from the telephone. For a while think about all the successes you've known. Think about all the blessings you enjoy. Think about all the things for which you can be thankful. Once you've done that, open your mind carefully, completely, and totally and write the answers to the following questions.

1. *I am excited about* . . . In complete detail write something you are excited about—something you have, you are, you're a part of, you believe in.
2. *I am grateful for* . . . List your blessings—all the things that you have to be thankful for, your family, your friends, your church, your work, your achievements, your awards, and so on. This will provide you with an escape from all the gloom, negativism, pessimism, and tragedy that you see in the world around you every day.
3. *I am interested in* . . . Here is where you will discover those things that can really turn you on in life. List the things you would *like* to do, *like* to have, *like* to be.
4. *I am confident of* . . . List your special talents and abilities and express your beliefs in what you know you can do, can have, can be.

An old Russian proverb says, "The very same hammer that shatters glass, forges steel." In other words, you can make out of your life whatever you want. You can allow tough times to defeat you and then give up and quit. Or you can look for an opportunity in each situation—an opportunity to do something different in your life—an opportunity to learn from your situation and grow into a better person. The choice is yours.

The point is that there is great *potential* in everyone. Your lists will show you just how much potential you have. The difference between the great and the mediocre, the powerful and the poor, the remembered and the forgotten, the successes and the failure lies in the choices people make during their lifetimes.

When life gets tough, when things really go bad, when nothing seems to work, we have three choices: 1. We can curse life for what it has done to us, look for a way to express our grief and rage, and then just give up altogether (as the 10 percent who fail). 2. We can grit our teeth, become martyrs, and simply "endure" (as the 80 percent who accept defeat, but do nothing about it). 3. Or we can accept what life has brought and look for ways to turn our crisis into an opportunity (as the 10 percent who succeed).

In 1960 two young Michigan brothers decided to go into business for themselves and bought a small pizza place with the intentions of building it into a successful business. But business didn't prove to be so good, and in 1965, when their partnership broke up, the business continued to flounder. Three years later a tragic fire consumed the majority of the business and the insurance company paid only ten cents on the dollar.

Undaunted, the remaining brother was determined not to give up and quit. He had faced tough times before. Orphaned at age four, he had spent the major portion of his life in various foster homes. He had held several odd jobs, including those of farmhand, pinsetter in a bowling alley, and newspaper boy. He had given up two attempts at college because of lack of finances and had spent four years in the marines during the turbulent sixties. He knew what adversity was. And he knew he had to begin again.

After struggling for two more years to make a go of his business, this young man faced foreclosure. In 1970, his bank and principal creditor took over the business. Ten months later the bank returned it to the owner in worse condition than when it had taken it. He now faced over fifteen hundred creditors, debts amounting to over $1.5 million, and more than a hundred lawsuits. The next few months and years would prove to be a real test of faith, patience, perseverance, and sheer courage. And he was willing to face those months and years with an expectation of success.

Tom Monahan, determined to overcome adversity and make it to the top, managed to rebuild his business, pay off all his creditors, and turn a small nondescript pizza place into one of the nation's largest pizza chains. He reintroduced home delivery to the American public, causing most of his competitors to follow suit. Today Domino's Pizza has over thirty-three hundred outlets across the nation and is rated among the fifty leading food-service organizations in America. All because one man refused to be defeated by adversity and looked to his future with hope.

There will be many times in life when we can't change the circumstances we face. But we can change how we *react* to those circumstances, always keeping in mind that there is a higher purpose for our struggle. That can make the difference between happiness and misery.

The caterpillars of a species of silkworm found in North America spin their cocoons among the branches of bushes and trees where they remain through the winter months until the transformed cecropia moths emerge in the spring. The cocoon breaks open to reveal a beautiful brown, orange, and gold moth within, slowly struggling to free itself from its prison. If an innocent passerby were to view this scene, he might feel tempted to slit the cocoon further and free the moth in hopes of alleviating its long struggle. However, what the passerby wouldn't know is that there is a higher purpose in the struggle of the cecropia moth slowly emerging from its cocoon.

As the moth struggles to free itself, it pushes its wings against the sides of the cocoon. The pressure of this action forces blood into the wing muscles, strengthening them in the process. Without that essential struggle, the moth would emerge with weak shriveled wings, unable to fly and it would become easy prey for a hungry predator. The crippled moth wouldn't survive even its first day of freedom.

The people who manage to flourish through adversity react positively to their circumstances—whatever they may be. They trust that there is a higher purpose for their struggle and try to find the good in each situation—to find the green shoots rising out of blackened ashes. They are willing to *persevere* until they get where they *desire* to go. They never offer excuses for their failures nor blame others for them. They accept responsibility for their mistakes and refuse to be discouraged and defeated. They keep coming back over and over again until they finally accomplish all they set out to accomplish. They know that the only time you fail is the very last time you try. And successful, persevering people never give up trying because they know *it's always too soon to quit!*

5

Enthusiasm and Dedication

One night years ago the screaming siren of a fire engine startled the residents of a small West Texas community out of their peaceful sleep. The volunteer fire department raced to the outskirts of town where they found the local Baptist church engulfed in flames. People came from all over town either to help fight the fire or to watch the burning church that most of them attended. They came dressed in robes thrown over pajamas and nightgowns and stood in their bedroom slippers to watch in sadness and awe as their church slowly disintegrated before their eyes.

The pastor of the church watched first the fire and then the faces in the crowd—most of whom were members of his congregation. As his eyes scanned the faces reflecting the brightness of the flames, he caught sight of a young man standing off to one side away from the crowd. The pastor hadn't seen this man before, so he walked over to introduce himself.

"I'm the pastor of this church," he said as he extended his hand in friendly greeting. "I don't think I've ever seen you at church before."

"Preacher," he responded, "this church has never been on fire before!"

Many people who have difficulties in life are lacking the "fire" it takes to overcome and succeed. They are lacking the third characteristic of successful people—*enthusiasm and dedication to a purpose.*

Enthusiasm derives from a Greek word that was originally used to describe religious fanaticism. Enthusiastic people have a passion and fervor that spills out of their lives and into others. They're enthusiastic because they care about themselves, other people, and what they're doing in life. They believe in their abilities and potential to do great things, but at the same time, they know it is their responsibility to utilize their abilities and activate their potential.

Charles Kingsley said, "We act as though comfort and luxury were the chief requirements of life, when all that we need to make us really happy is something to be enthusiastic about."

Thomas Carlyle said that every man is enthusiastic at some time in life—some for an hour and some for a day. But the one who is successful is the one who can become enthusiastic and stay that way.

John Wesley, founder of the Methodist Church, was a small man, weighing about 127 pounds. He would rise at 5:00 A.M. every day and ride horseback through the English countryside, seeking out people to hear his message. Some days he would ride up to sixty miles—quite an accomplishment back then. Midnight would find him still preaching, still energetic, still enthusiastic and unexhausted.

History tells us that twelve thousand people once heard John Wesley preach. Those twelve thousand came by foot, by oxcart, horseback, and carriage. They came all day long to hear the little man who could spark enthusiasm in everyone who heard him.

Once, an excited man was so touched by Wesley's message that he rushed through the crowd, grabbed Wesley, and said, "Dr. Wesley, you're a phenomenal speaker. Thousands came here today to hear you speak. What's your secret?"

"I don't know, son," he answered. "I just set John Wesley on fire, and people come to see him burn!"[1]

John Wesley had a contagious enthusiasm for his work that radiated from him as he spoke. He possessed dedication to and singleness of purpose. He had a goal to work toward and the self-confidence and the burning desire to do whatever was necessary to accomplish it. His enthusiasm and dedication to his purpose enabled him to become a great instrument in the Lord's work.

Another Methodist itinerant evangelist, William Booth, found his destiny in preaching to the poor, the lost, and the homeless of the London slums. Here he, his wife, Catherine, and their eight children endured the hardships of cold, hunger, and abuse while they ran their East London "Christian Mission." The Booths founded the mission in 1865 and thirteen years later changed its name to the Salvation Army when a military organization with its terminology, uniforms, and martial music were found to be effective in attracting neglected slum dwellers. Today, the Salvation Army stands as a monument, not only to its great founder, but also to his enthusiastic and dedicated wife who worked beside him and sacrificed so much for the sake of their work.

Catherine Booth, chronically ill since childhood, suffered from curvature of the spine, tuberculosis, and, toward the end of her life, the torments of cancer. Catherine confessed on her deathbed that she had never known a day without pain. Yet, this frail, delicate woman not only cooked, washed, and cared for her husband and their eight children, but she also aided him in his merciful efforts for those poorer than they. In the evening after her day's labors, Catherine would eagerly search the East London slums for people who were hungry, homeless, ill, or in trouble. She organized soup kitchens and homes for unmarried mothers, and she preached sermons on the streets to thieves and prostitutes.

One day a council of ministers, impressed with William Booth's sincerity, offered him a comfortable pulpit in a well-to-do parish on the condition that he would give up his work in the slums. One would think that Catherine, after living in poverty for so long, would have jumped at any chance to get away from all the depravity. Instead, upon hearing the generous offer, Catherine exclaimed, "Never! Never!" Her husband felt the same.

The "Church of the Churchless" spread throughout the British Isles and around the world through the dedicated and enthusiastic efforts of William and Catherine Booth. Merely fifteen years after it was founded, the Salvation Army began service in the United States and later won recognition for bringing religion to the city slums and for its work with American forces during World War I. Its program of social activities included homes and hospitals for unwed mothers, shelters and rehabilitation centers for homeless men and women, youth programs, prison work, and emergency disaster services.

Thanks to the fearless, unfaltering, dedicated, and enthusiastic Booths, the Salvation Army is still marching today. It has since grown into an international religious and social welfare organization providing services in over eighty countries for all persons, regardless of race, color, religion, or depth of depravity.

The English people knew the contribution that these two people had made to the world. When William Booth died, sixty-five thousand people thronged the streets of London to pay homage to him as his funeral procession, which included the lord mayor of London, solemnly marched by. The royal houses of Europe and the president of the United States sent flowers. Thousands of members of the Salvation Army marched behind his coffin singing hymns in honor of their fallen first general. I would like to think that Catherine, who died before her husband and who had spurned security in order to take part in a greater cause, somehow knew the homage that the world paid them both.

Everything you have ever experienced in life—the bad as well as the good—serves to prepare you for that magic moment when you, like William and Catherine Booth, can leave behind a mark others can look to for hope.

I know what you're thinking. You're thinking that it's easy for some people to be enthusiastic, but not for you. Maybe you've lost your flame of enthusiasm because of some disability or handicap. Maybe you wonder how you can be enthusiastic when you have no income, when there's illness in your family, when your child is in trouble, when you can't pay your bills, when you've lost your job, or when you've lost a loved one.

• Lord Byron and John Keats had a clubfoot and tuberculosis respectively. Yet they became two of the most respected of the world's poets. Beethoven, in spite of his deafness, composed some of the most beautiful music to ever fall upon human ears. And Julius Caesar, one of the greatest emperors of Rome, suffered from epilepsy.

• Judy Martin runs a successful business from her home out of which she works as a consultant, special projects coordinator, and art broker. She directs various cultural projects, coordinates memorial programs, and produces art shows and various community events. What makes Judy such a special person, aside from the fact that she has built a successful business from the ground up, is that she runs that business from her bed.

Judy's legs became paralyzed in 1978 from a muscular disease. When a well-meaning social worker got her a job at minimum wage grading papers, Judy decided to prove that her physical condition had nothing whatsoever to do with her intellectual ability. She knew she could still hold down a professional job. Her determination and dedication to this purpose enabled her to start her own company.

But Judy would rather talk about her accomplishments than her disability: She has coordinated three citywide memorial programs and has served as a consultant for a conference on black people with disabilities sponsored by her state governor's Committee for Disabled Persons. Judy maintains an enthusiasm and a dedication for her work that transcends any disability she may have.

• One of the federal government's programs suffered some unfortunate setbacks in recent years which resulted in discouragement and defeat among the loyal and dedicated people of that organization. Hoping to give these deserving people a shot in the arm, the government decided to give an award to the outstanding administrator within the program.

Sally Phillips, the recipient of the award was the nineteenth child in a black family from a small town in the Southwest. The day of her birth, Sally's callous and unfeeling doctor placed her in a shoe box, covered it with a lid, and told her mother she didn't want the baby.

"Yes, I do!" her mother cried. "I *do* want my baby!"

"Not this baby," said the doctor. "She has no hands and only short little nubs for arms. She won't be able to survive in the outside world. She's better off in an institution with people who will care for her for the rest of her life."

"No!" the mother insisted. "I want my baby!"

Sally's mother took her away from the doctor and lovingly cared for her, nurtured her, and taught her how to survive in an uncaring and cruel world. When she was six years old, Sally started to school with her peers. The first day of school her teacher sent her home with a note pinned to her cotton dress which read, "We have no place for a handicapped child in this school."

Outraged and determined to obtain an education for her child, Sally's mother marched her back to the school and demanded, "My child *will* go to school here. She is *not* handicapped. She just has a little problem."

Thanks to her mother's endless determination, Sally completed elementary school, junior high school, and high school in her small hometown. Then she went on to college where she earned both a bachelor's and a master's degree, and finally her doctorate. Today she has a rewarding career, drives her own car, and pilots an airplane.

The day Sally received the outstanding administrator award from her employer, thousands of fellow employees and invited guests gave her a standing ovation. Tears rolled down their faces as they watched her walk across the stage and reach out to take her award with the hooks she has in the place of hands. Sally Phillips was not just dedicated to becoming all she ever dreamed of becoming. Her award testifies to the fact that she still continues to strive to be the very best she can be, to be enthusiastic about her work, and to be dedicated and committed to a purpose.

Dr. David McClellan, after twenty-five years of research, says that singleness of purpose is the one factor that will help us cope with all the questions and problems of life. Studies show that there are thirty-one major reasons people fail and thirteen major ways to be successful. The reason heading each list is singleness of purpose: You fail without a goal in your life and you succeed if you have total commitment and dedication to a purpose. This dedication gives people the motivation to *act* and do the things necessary to overcome hardships and obstacles.

Maybe you don't yet know your purpose in life. But you do know your talents and abilities. You do know what you can do best. Use that to your advantage by doing something positive and fruitful. Because the value of your life is determined by what you do with what you have.

A bar of iron lying in a junkyard would be worth about five dollars in raw form. The same iron, however, could be processed and made into other objects far more valuable. Its value lies in the purpose for which it's used:

* horseshoes—$10
* steam engine—$23
* mould-board for a plow—$50
* scissors—$83
* needles—$8,300
* surgical instruments—$33,000
* balance springs for watches—$166,000

Perhaps you feel it's just not the right time in your life for you to achieve your dream. Maybe you think it's either too soon or too late. Perhaps you agree with the many people who come up to me after I speak and tell me things like, "I know, Lewis, you have a point. I probably should have a purpose in my life. *But*, I'm too old now to start all over. I had my chance and I blew it."

Behind that person comes the younger man or woman who says, "Gee, Lewis, I can hardly wait until I get older. I'm just too young to do anything meaningful. I must build up my business first. It's going to take time."

As these people walk away, I wonder why I didn't tell

them that William Pitt the Younger, because of his ability and self-confidence, became prime minister of Great Britain at age twenty-four. Gladstone became prime minister at age fifty-nine and served for six years, after which he temporarily retired. Six years after that, he reentered politics, again won the election, and became prime minister for the second time at age seventy-one. I should have mentioned to them that Sir Isaac Newton discovered the law of gravity when he was only twenty-three and Galileo built the first pendulum clock after he had reached his seventies and *after* he'd lost his sight.

Somehow I should have told them that Charles Lindbergh conquered the Atlantic Ocean at age twenty-four and P. T. Barnum didn't even enter the circus world until age sixty-one. Percy Bysshe Shelley had written all of his works and died before the age of thirty. J. P. Morgan, one of the greatest financiers of all time, was not a financial success until after age fifty. And Alexander the Great conquered the world and died before he was thirty-three. *It's always too soon to quit, and it's never too late to begin.*

Ben Woodson once said, "The longer I live, the more firmly convinced I become that the essential factor that sets one man apart from his fellow men in terms of success is *dedication to achieve.*"

Several years ago I read a story about a group of whales that, while pursuing sardines, found themselves marooned in a small bay—a bay that proved to be a death trap for the large mammals. Frederick Brown Harris commented, "The small fish lured the sea giants to their deaths. . . . They came to their violent demise by chasing small ends, by prostituting vast powers for insignificant goals."

Such is true of human beings as well. Without a meaningful, significant purpose, life becomes a deadly, dull existence. Then during the times of testing, our will to fight on is lessened and we often give up and quit.

Viktor Frankl spent several years in a concentration camp during World War II. He says that the prisoner who lost faith in the future—faith in his aims and goals for his life—was doomed. "With his loss of belief in the future," Frankl said, "he also lost his spiritual hold; he let himself decline and become subject to mental and physical decay."

The temptation to be discouraged is common to every man or woman. Discouragement is no respecter of persons. Don't allow discouragement and the chasing of "small ends" cause you to give up and quit.

Before I became a professional speaker, I served as president of an insurance company. One day a young man came into my office to apply for a job. Although I wasn't currently in the market for a new salesman, I agreed to conduct an interview. I heard very little of what this man had to say during the interview. I couldn't get past how he looked and acted. He was a small, skinny man with tousled hair. He wore rumpled clothing and very thick eyeglasses. Shy and withdrawn, he didn't seem like the kind of assertive outgoing person it takes to meet the public on a daily basis. So I was greatly surprised when he told me he wanted to be the world's greatest insurance salesman.

"I'm sorry," I told him. "I just don't have any openings at this time."

Four years later I sold my company and began speaking full-time. One morning a young man came into my office to see me. He stood erect and presented an impression of authority and confidence. His clothes were neat and clean and his hair was groomed to perfection. He looked good, and he even smelled good. At first glance, I thought he looked vaguely familiar, but I couldn't place where I'd seen him before.

"I still want to be the world's greatest insurance salesman," he said.

I know my chin must have hit my knees when I finally realized who this man was. I couldn't believe my eyes. He had obviously meant what he told me four years earlier. And he had somehow found out all the things he needed to accomplish his goal. Anyone with that kind of dedication and commitment would make an excellent employee.

"I'm not in the insurance business anymore," I told him. "I sold my business. But I have a friend in the business who may be able to help you out."

I phoned my friend and arranged for him to interview

this young man—an interview that resulted in his employment. That was approximately fifteen years ago. By 1986 that dedicated young man had sold over one *billion* dollars' worth of life insurance. The secret to his success? Enthusiasm about his work and dedication and commitment to a purpose.

Enthusiastic, dedicated people are motivated to *act*. They are the doers of the world. They are excited about life and want to be in the middle of it. They have a singleness of purpose on which they focus—a purpose consistent with God's leading and their natural talents. They are dedicated to working toward and achieving that purpose or goal. There is power in the life of a person who has an expectation, a commitment, a dedication, and a willingness to pay the price to accomplish all he or she desires and deserves.

That kind of singleness of purpose can be found in the short life of Terry Fox. After losing his leg to cancer, this young Canadian felt an inner drive and dedication to raise a million dollars for cancer research by *running* across Canada. Although he overcame overwhelming odds in attempting this great feat, cancer later invaded his lungs and eventually took his life. But Terry Fox's dedication fired the hearts of millions of Canadians and Americans alike who donated *$20 million* to his cause.

Enthusiastic and dedicated people set goals that help them concentrate all their power, energy, and talent in one direction. They have learned the lesson of the magnifying glass. It captures the sun's rays, harnesses its power, focuses its energy, and brings forth fire. That's exactly what a commitment to a purpose will do. It can capture your potential, harness your talent, focus your energy, and bring forth accomplishment.

The king salmon hatches in the fresh water rivers of the northwestern United States. After the female salmon lays approximately thirty thousand eggs deep within the gravel of a riverbed, she swims away with her mate to die. The young salmon will survive off the nourishment within each yolk sac until they are old enough and large enough to fend for themselves. The survival rate among the young salmon is only 5 to 10 percent.

Once the young salmon have exhausted the nourishment in their yolk sacs, they rise above the gravel bed and are swept by the river current into a nearby lake. Here they feed on insects and plankton until they reach maturity. Once mature they swim out to sea to spend from one to four years swimming in the saltwater of the Pacific Ocean.

At the end of their four-year stay in the ocean, a strange thing happens. The salmon begin returning to the waters in which they were hatched. Possessing a unique ability to scent its own spawning grounds, the king salmon will swim through the ocean until it reaches the mouth of the river in which it was born. Its dedication to this purpose is so intense that it will attempt to surpass overwhelming odds in order to achieve its goal.

In seeking its birthplace, the salmon must first swim upstream against the current, sometimes finding it necessary to *leap* up and over strong waterfalls. In addition, it must avoid predators such as bear and birds searching for a meal. In its quest for home, the king salmon travels approximately twenty-five miles per day. If it is lucky enough to reach home without succumbing to one of the many hazards of the long journey, it will then lay its own eggs, beginning the cycle once again.

The king salmon exemplifies the kind of dedication to purpose we must maintain if we are to overcome the many obstacles and hazards in our own paths. Dedication and commitment to a purpose will help you concentrate all your effort on an end result about which you're excited and enthusiastic. That end result will give you the strength and courage to persevere when the going gets rough. It will help build your self-confidence, giving you a sense of personal achievement and self-fulfillment.

The value of what you do in life lies in the purpose to which you're dedicated. You can use your driving ability to steer a getaway car in a bank robbery, or you can drive fifty children to church on a bus on Sunday mornings. It isn't what you are that matters, but rather what you do with what you have. Dr. Peter Marshall said, "The true measure of life is not its duration, but its donation." Yours could be the tiny voice that makes the difference provided you have enthusiasm, dedication, and commitment.

All the enthusiastic people I have ever met were enthusiastic because they were doing what they loved to do most, because they were dedicated and committed to a purpose greater than they. I realize that it isn't always possible to do what you love most. Sometimes we must take whatever job we can find in order to put food on the table. But examine your inner self—your values, your talents and abilities, and your own confidence. Perhaps you feel as some people who don't *want* to find a better job because they're afraid the challenge will be so great that they'll fail. Mary Crowley pointed this out in an interview by using the following story:

An industrial expert went around asking different people about their jobs.

A girl was running a machine and he asked, "What do you like best about your job?"

"The good pay," she said.

"What do you like least about your job?"

"The good pay," she said again.

He was surprised. "What do you mean? You like it the best and you like it the least?"

"Well, I like it because it pays me well, so that's the good part. But if it didn't pay so well, I'd quit this dumb job!"[2]

If you don't like your job, find some aspect of it that you do enjoy, or for which you can be thankful and concentrate on that. Have the courage to explore new possibilities and make changes in the unpleasant situations in your life. Remain confident in yourself and in your talents and abilities to believe that victory will come.

Having confidence in yourself doesn't mean that you become self-centered or egotistical. It simply means that you can develop a confidence in and enthusiasm for your God-given talents and abilities, refusing to accept defeat and claiming responsibility when you fail. It means that you accept yourself for what you are and are confident that you can do whatever you set your heart and mind on. This attitude will enable you to have an enthusiasm and a dedication for your work, your goals, and your dreams which, like that of John Wesley, will be contagious.

As I have said earlier, you wouldn't have a special talent and a love and desire for something if it wasn't possible for you to have it. Perhaps a hobby can slowly be built into a thriving business to the point where you can eventually give up that job you don't particularly like. Perhaps you can go back to school part-time to get that law degree you've always craved. If you have a desire for something that corresponds with the talents God has given you, you won't have to worry about the enthusiasm and dedication. Because if you're willing to flourish through the adversity, then the enthusiasm and dedication will come without fail. Don't give up seeking your dream because *it's always too soon to quit!*

6

Attitude That Expects to Succeed

During the 1984 summer Olympics in Los Angeles, a small (four foot nine) fifteen-year-old American gymnast won the hearts of Americans. Because of her performance and that of her teammates, the United States sat on the verge of winning gold medals in women's gymnastics—a category so long dominated by the Communist bloc nations.

Americans watched breathlessly as Mary Lou Retton readied herself for her final event. The vault would make or break her championship. A mere half point behind the first-place gymnast, Mary Lou stood in the spotlight in front of the rolling cameras and cheering crowd and concentrated on the vault before her. All of a sudden, as if the vault emitted a secret signal, she dipped her head in a quick, almost imperceptible nod, smiled, and then bounded down the path to complete her event. Mary Lou Retton scored a perfect 10! Then, to everyone's amazement, and as if to prove that the first vault wasn't a mistake, she took a second vault and scored *another* perfect 10!

Mary Lou later told reporters that while she stood before the vault contemplating her goal, she had simply run the exercise over and over in her mind, visualizing every perfect step. Then when she actually executed it, it came easily for her. Her coach had taught her to *never be surprised to win!*[1] Mary Lou possesses what I believe to be the fourth characteristic of successful people: *an attitude that expects to succeed.*

Unlike people of past centuries who didn't have the opportunity to witness much change, we have gone from horse-drawn carriages to space travel within a short span of fifty years. Although there will always be prophets of doom, we *know* what can be achieved with a little effort and ingenuity. We *know* that those who succeed are those who are willing to look beyond today and imagine other possibilities.

This is an exciting time just to be alive. There have been some miraculous developments within the past few decades. We can only imagine the amazing things waiting for us tomorrow.

• Man's knowledge is increasing at the explosive rate of half a million pages per minute! This means that the average scientist or engineer will soon have to devote one day per week to formal education in order to keep up in his or her field.

• Air travel has accelerated from six miles per hour to twenty-five thousand miles per hour since man's first flight in 1903.

• A machine currently exists that can produce the findings of twelve different chemical tests from one sample of blood in merely twelve minutes.

• An optical scanner can process the quarterly earnings statements of 3.5 million employees in only one day—a task that would require a man thirteen weeks to accomplish by hand.

• Tests are currently being conducted on an experimental washing machine that can wash, dry, and iron a sheet within forty-five seconds. This could revolutionize the laundry industry.

• Lasers are powerful beams of light that have a purity and precision a million times greater than that of ordinary light. The first laser was made in 1960. Within the next twenty-seven years, scientists discovered a myriad of uses for this versatile invention. Lasers have been used to burn tiny holes through diamonds and metals, weld detached retinas to the eye without surgery, bounce light off the moon with even better results than radar, measure both time and distance with extreme accuracy, and produce three-dimensional photographs that you can see *around*. (And you thought that was only possible in *Star Wars!*)

We live in a time when we witness success on a daily basis. We know the possibilities when man applies himself to a task that is seemingly greater than his abilities. That alone should give us an expectation of success. But we've also seen a lot of devastation, tragedy, and failure in life and these things cause people to fear the unknown.

What a horrible and deadly disease fear is! Fear is the basis for most superstitions. Superstitious people won't walk under ladders, allow black cats to cross their paths, or leave their homes on Friday the thirteenth for fear of bad luck coming their way. But fear has much more severe effects on people than the development of little superstitious habits.

Research at the University of Colorado revealed that the inability to cope with fear may weaken the body's immune system. This study concluded that "among tuberculosis victims, the onset of the disease usually follows a cluster of disruptive events." *Fear gives more pain than does the pain it fears*. Fear and stress take a phenomenal toll on the health and lives of people who allow it to control them.

• After a resounding defeat for a third-term governorship, New Hampshire's Governor Hugh Gallen promptly contracted a "mysterious blood infection" and died.

• British car manufacturer Colin Chapman, under vigorous criticism by stockholders, suffered a heart attack and died at age fifty-four.

• Chicago's Cardinal Cody, under investigation for diverting church money to a woman, lived less than one year after the investigation began.

• Al Bloomingdale, disgraced by his secretly "kept woman," lived less than one month after this scandal became public.

Throughout the Bible we find references indicating that fear is unhealthy. The Scriptures state over three hundred and fifty times that we must "fear not." Yet we heed not. If I tell myself each day that I can't handle a specific job, that I'll never make it, that I'm destined to be a nobody, then that is exactly what I'll be. If you're programing yourself negatively by expecting failure, those negative thoughts will eventually translate to your subconscious mind as well as into your physical body. The subconscious mind believes what it's told, so it will cause you to act in such way as to bring about those very things you fear the most.[2]

Life is very much a self-fulfilling prophecy as Dr. James says. I'm sure you've known people who do nothing but complain about *everything*. Most of the time these people are not successful. Usually they're the people who go nowhere in their jobs, have no ambition, and never try anything new. Their negative attitude keeps them bound in a negative life. People may blame their lack of success on many things, one of which may be not enough education. Many people have succeeded in life without formal educations and many who were thought to be intellectually inferior have proved their teachers and critics wrong.

• Henry Ford had only six months of formal schooling when he began his career as a bicycle mechanic.

• Thomas Edison's teacher told his mother that her eleven-year-old son was "too dumb to learn." Evidently they forgot to tell Edison because the contributions his inventions have made to society testify to his genius.

• The parents of Albert Einstein thought he was mentally disturbed because he didn't talk until he was three years old. Perhaps Einstein was simply waiting until he had something worthwhile to say.

• Harry S. Truman was turned down by West Point. But he refused to believe himself a failure and went on to become president of the United States.

While some people blame their failure to achieve on lack of education, others may blame their situations on their race, creed, color, religion, or disability. They may think successful people are exceptions. These people haven't had other problems to overcome. They haven't been looked down upon because they're different from others. They haven't been frowned upon, laughed at, or discriminated against.

• Benjamin Disraeli, a Christian of Jewish descent, grew up in an age of great prejudice against his race. But, in spite of the prejudices of others, Disraeli maintained a confident expectation of success, often stating that he felt he was a man of destiny. Although poorly educated, he established a reputation as an author at the early age of twenty-two, and continued to write acclaimed works until his death.

Disraeli began in politics at thirty-three by entering Parliament where he gained a great reputation as an orator and party whip. He became prime minister in 1868 and was known for his foreign policy and as a champion of the working classes. Truly living up to his early vision that he was a man of destiny, Disraeli accomplished great things during his career—among them were recognition of the trade unions, public health reform, and housing legislation for the poor.

• Booker T. Washington was born the mulatto son of a slave mother in Virginia. Although the slaves were given their freedom when he was only three years old, he spent a great part of his early life in child labor, working in the salt furnaces and coal mines of West Virginia. When he was seventeen, Washington walked five hundred miles to Hampton Agricultural Institute in Virginia to begin his education. At nineteen he graduated and went to Tuskegee, Alabama, to begin his teaching career. There he became the founder and head of Tuskegee Institute where he devoted the rest of his life to Negro education.

• George Washington Carver was born into slavery in Missouri. While an infant he was kidnapped and then ransomed back by his original owner for a $300 racehorse. His thirst for knowledge led him to work his way through school and he earned a bachelor's and a master's degree from Iowa State College of Agriculture and Mechanic Arts. This was quite an achievement for a black man living in the nineteenth century.

Carver later became head of the agriculture department at Tuskegee Institute where he both taught and conducted research. He is most noted for his work with peanuts and sweet potatoes, from which developed hundreds of useful products. He served as a consultant to the United States Bureau of Plant Industry and received many awards for his contributions to agricultural science.

• America watched TV news reports in wonder when a set of German Siamese twins, joined at the head, were separated at Johns Hopkins Hospital in 1987. Shortly after that miraculous separation, Geraldo Rivera had two sets of Siamese twins on his TV show along with the doctor who had separated one set eight years earlier. One of the two sets of twins, Yvette and Yvonne McCarther, have not been separated. The two smiling sisters sat next to each other with their heads, joined at the top, lying to one side on their shoulders. Currently attending college, the sisters said they wanted to be nurses.

"Can you imagine our résumés?" one asked. "We'll have to tell an employer he has to hire *two!*" Then they both burst into laughter.

When Rivera asked about their quality of life, they both responded in unison, "Life is great."

• When Pope John Paul II visited the United States in September 1987, he enjoyed the music of a young Mexican-American singer and guitarist from California. Tony Melendez's beautiful voice rang with confidence, love, hope, and, most of all, dignity. Tony was born with no arms to a mother who took thalidomide during her pregnancy (a prescription drug now banned by the Food & Drug Administration because it has caused serious birth defects). Visibly moved, the audience watched and listened in awe-struck silence as this courageous young man poured out his heart in song and strummed his guitar with his *toes.* The words of his song say it all:

Life passes by too quickly
To allow a little problem
To get you down.

What sets these people apart from others is their attitude—their dedication, determination, and expectation of success in spite of their differences and any other drawbacks they may have. Dr. James said that the greatest discovery of his generation is that man can change his destiny simply by changing his attitude. In other words, *your attitude, not your aptitude, determines your altitude.* This is a fact that has always been true even though many couldn't—and some still don't—believe it.

I read of a college professor who questioned the philosophy that only those people with positive attitudes are revered in life. After all, there's never been a monument built to a cynic—not that I know of anyway. So this professor, hoping to expose this philosophy as false, borrowed the college track team for a few days for an experiment. The professor divided the team into two equal groups—equal in their number, in their abilities, in their physical stamina, and so on. When he finished, he was satisfied that the two teams were matched as completely as possible.

The professor then took the first team to the track and told them that they would be given a series of scientific tests as part of a study being conducted by the school. The purpose of the tests, he told them, would be to measure physical strength and endurance, agility, and physical stamina. He went on to tell the men that he wasn't sure they could complete the tests because they were extremely difficult. But, he told them, they must try to do the very best they could. The team members took the tests and tried to do their best, but 57 percent couldn't complete them.

Then the professor took the second team to the track. This time he told the men the same thing he told the first team—that the tests were extremely difficult and he didn't think they could master them. But this time he added something new. He told the men that one of the labs at the school had developed a new pill that had a tremendous capacity to increase a person's endurance, strength, stamina, agility, and ability to perform. This time he said the purpose for the tests was to prove the power of this amazing new pill.

The team members willingly took what they didn't know to be salt tablets and proceeded to take the tests. Eighty-eight percent not only completed the tests, but, in some cases, broke records that they had previously held. When the professor wrote up the results of his study with the track team, he said, "I must learn one of two things from this test. Either there are some unusual properties in salt that I never knew about before or there is truth to the idea that what your mind can believe, you can achieve." People can change their destinies by changing their attitude.

A few years ago I had the privilege of listening to a man who some had thought at one time to be a failure. Fired from his previous job, he now headed a company that was technically bankrupt. Those he spoke to that day—many of whom were his employees—didn't really know him, but they, like myself, found themselves caught up in his honesty, courage, and belief. There was not one doubt in his mind that his company would revive, that times would be good again, that the company would bounce back and be better than ever before.

"Follow me and I'll bring you back," he said.

Upon hearing these words, individuals in the audience looked at one another, and laughingly said, "Sure you will." The employees' skepticism didn't go unnoticed. Not only did the employees of his company laugh at this man, but also members of the press who were there covering the meeting. Their skepticism was evident the next day in the newspapers.

I was so impressed by this man's expectation of success that I couldn't get him out of my mind. I could see that he had what it takes to make it. His enthusiasm was contagious. In fact, I was so impressed with him that I went home to Austin and called my broker to buy stock in his failing company. I knew it would come back. My broker laughed at me. He tried to discourage me from buying the stock, saying the company was going down the tubes. But I wouldn't be discouraged.

My broker hadn't heard that man speak. I did hear him, and I *knew* he would make it. I could see his enthusiasm and hope as he stood before the audience and told them that even though he'd been fired from his previous company after thirty-three years of service, now, at age fifty-two, he looked forward to beginning again, to starting anew.

"I've been up and I've been down," he said. "And now I'm coming back up again."

The rest of the story is history. Under the positive leadership of Lee Iaccoca, Chrysler Corporation not only recovered from near bankruptcy, but it also came back as a strong company which eventually bought out American Motors to become one of the most successful businesses in the nation. What made the difference? One man's positive attitude, expectation for success, contagious enthusiasm, and dedication to purpose, which in turn infected and affected the employees of his company. For the first time in a long time they had hope and a purpose for which to work.

I once made a speech at Sea Island, Georgia. It is one of the most beautiful places I have ever visited. Mile after mile of flat white sandy beaches border the blue waters of the Atlantic Ocean. All along the beaches I saw dozens upon dozens of sand boats which are small boatlike vehicles mounted on wheels. Visitors to the beaches can rent these boats and sail them up and down the beaches. If a person wants to go south on the beach, he sets the sail a particular way so the wind can fill out the sail and send the boat flying down the beach at twenty to thirty miles per hour. However, if he wants to go north on the beach, he merely sets the sail another way and the wind will send the boat north.

As I watched these sand boats flying past one another at combined speeds reaching fifty to sixty miles per hour, I realized that the same wind blowing in one direction was propelling these boats in two separate directions—some north and some south. The *attitude* of the sail made all the difference.

One great thrill of my life came when I had the privilege of sharing a program with a young man whom I believe to be one of the greatest football players of all time. The professional football leagues thought he was so good that they tried to recruit him during his junior year in college. He refused because he dreamed of leading his team to the Rose Bowl, and he wanted to see that dream come true. In his senior year he led his team to a winning season, to the Rose Bowl that January, and to a national championship. He then went on to win the Heisman Trophy as the best college football player in the country and thus became the number-one draft choice for professional football.

Jim Plunkett's parents were both blind and could never watch their son play football. For much of the early part of his life his family lived on welfare. He grew up facing the prejudices that went with his Mexican-American heritage. But Jim Plunkett never let the adversity in his life keep him from maintaining a wholesome positive attitude. He looked at life with courage and with hope and with an expectation for achievement.

Dr. Norman Cousins, former editor of the acclaimed *Saturday Review,* was hospitalized in the early 1960s with an extremely crippling disease that his doctors said had no cure. Acutely aware of the harmful effects that negative emotions can have on humans, Dr. Cousins reasoned that the reverse must also be true—positive feelings, thoughts, and emotions can have a positive healing effect. So he borrowed a movie projector and prescribed his own treatment by introducing humor and laughter into his daily regimen.

For hours each day, Dr. Cousins watched old Marx Brothers films, "Candid Camera" reruns, and other films that made him laugh. He also studied all aspects of his disease and with the help of his physicians learned what had to take place within his ailing body before it could become healthy again.

Dr. Cousins wrote about his unique experience in his book *Anatomy of an Illness as Perceived by the Patient.* In it he wrote that he made the joyous discovery that ten minutes of genuine belly laughter would give him at least two hours of pain-free sleep each day. What had seemed to be a progressively debilitating and fatal cellular disease was eventually reversed and in time Norman Cousins recovered completely.

Since Dr. Cousins's miraculous recovery, scientists at the University of Colorado have discovered evidence supporting his findings. During laughter the brain releases chemicals that have a pain-reducing and healing quality. However, another chemical, released from the brain during periods of intense stress and fear, *blocks* the healing chemicals, thus setting a person up for long-term illness.

Many physicians and scientists now believe Dr. Cousins recovered because the healthy positive attitude he maintained throughout had a healing effect on his body. He didn't give in to his disease and allow it to control his emotions. He tried to control the disease instead. He didn't become depressed and make out a will. He looked beyond his problem to possible solutions and tried to learn everything he could about his disease so he could *fight* it with a positive attitude and an expectation of recovery.

Instead of expecting failure, you must look at life positively—look for solutions to problems, look for the good in each bad situation, expect to succeed at the things you attempt. In so doing, you will increase your capacity for living. Gandhi once said, "Man often becomes what he believes." You must believe in yourself and in God and make a decision to change your attitude and expect the best from life. And when the best doesn't come along, you must look for ways to make each situation better.

One of my British friends once told me that Winston Churchill believed that if he could change the way a person saw a situation he could change the way that person behaved in that particular situation. One of the reasons Churchill made his famous radio talks during World War II was to paint a picture that would enable the English people to see the war in a more positive light. He wanted them to believe in their country and maintain courage and an expectation for victory.

My friend's father owned a shop in downtown London. Each morning during World War II, his father unlocked the door to his shop and hung out a sign that read Open for Business. Then the bombs came. Havoc reigned as the courage and hopes of the English people were dashed against the rubble of what remained of London. When they emerged from the bomb shelters, the English people found their city ravaged, burned, and broken. Homes, churches, office buildings, and shops were devastated. Father and son returned to the site of their shop to find the entire front of their store gone.

"For the first time in my life," he said, "I saw my father cry."

He told me how his father's face fell, his shoulders drooped, and tears flowed down his face. The father disappeared into the back of the store and sat staring into empty space. Suddenly the radio began to crackle and pop, and above the static the rich voice of Winston Churchill could be heard speaking to his beloved English people.

"We're going to fight them on the seas. We're going to fight them in the country. We're going to fight them in the streets. **We shall never give up!**"

The father sat up erect and a faraway look veiled his eyes. The tears dried up and his eyes became bright again. He arose from his chair and returned to the front of his store, digging through the rubble until he found the objects of his search. He vigorously painted a new sign and, when he finished, hung it on a broken board in front of his store. It read **MORE** Open for Business!

What changed? One minute this man was broken and defeated. The very next minute he was enthusiastic, encouraged, and hopeful. The situation didn't change; nothing at all changed *except his attitude*. Churchill was right. He was able, with a few encouraging words, to change the way one man saw a particular situation. And from the way the English people rallied during the war, this English merchant wasn't the only person who benefited from Churchill's psychology. His encouraging words, heard regularly on his radio broadcasts, changed the way an entire *country* viewed the war.

One spring morning around eleven I arrived in Birmingham, Alabama. Scheduled to speak at 7:00 P.M., I had over half a day to kill. My host invited me to play golf with him and some of his friends. Eager to spend a relaxing afternoon before my speech, I borrowed golf shoes and clubs and joined them at the golf course. When I arrived, I was thrilled to learn that my playing partner would be Charlie Boswell. That day I learned a lot about this amazing man.

Charlie played football in college and was captain of the winning football team of the 1937 Rose Bowl. During World War II, while he was serving as captain in the infantry, a land mine exploded and he lost his eyesight. But I played nine holes of golf with Charlie Boswell. Charlie's caddie would explain the lay of the land, the slope of the green, the obstacles in his way, and so on. Then he would rattle a pin in the cup so Charlie could *hear* the direction of the sound. Then Charlie would make the appropriate shot. For nine holes of golf I watched a man who couldn't see shoot *par* golf. How did he do that?

When I asked him how he managed to play better than I could with all my five senses, Charlie said he *visualized in his mind what he had to do.* Like Mary Lou Retton, he saw what he had to do and then he did it—with the expectation of success! Be careful of what you expect, because you're probably going to get it.

In 1980 the Pacific Northwest shuddered under the devastating force of the eruption of Mount Saint Helens. Television and newspapers reported that forests had been annihilated, rivers choked, fish and wildlife destroyed, and the air poisoned. They ominously predicted that acid rain clouds would form and weather patterns could be permanently changed. This influenced the attitudes of the inhabitants of the Northwest as they prepared for a bleak future.

Less than one year after the eruption, scientists studying the area discovered that in spite of the fact that the rivers had been clogged with hot mud, volcanic ash, and floating debris, the salmon and steelhead had somehow miraculously managed to survive by following *alternate* streams home, some of which were less than six-inches deep. Fields, lakes, and rivers surrounding Mount Saint Helens soon teemed with wildlife and plant life again, their waters and soil full of rich life-supporting nutrients generously supplied by the exploding volcano.

The expectations and hopes of the local inhabitants slowly began to change. They were seeing the signs of new hope and new life that they thought had been lost for many years to come. Farmers whose crops were wiped out by the thick layer of ash soon discovered they were in possession of rich mineral deposits that would supply life-giving food to years of future crops. Mount Saint Helens had unwittingly done her part to repair the damage she had wrought. Remember, trouble isn't always trouble.

How can a person maintain an attitude that expects to succeed in the face of disaster and tragedy? Again, this is an act of will. But it takes practice. It's simply a matter of establishing a new habit through repetitive *actions*.

If you want to develop a new attitude, you have to remember to:

1. *Begin each day on a positive note.* Because the way you begin the day is the way you go through the day. If you have the habit of slapping the snooze button on your alarm clock fifteen times and sleeping an extra thirty minutes each morning, break it. The radio clicks on and you listen to the news—inflation, murder, robbery, rape, assault. Don't begin your day that way. Don't grumble about the day you must face. Half the battle is won if you're just *up*, so jump out of bed on the *first* ring of the alarm—even if you have to put the clock on the opposite side of the room in order to get out of bed. The important thing is to begin a repetitive action that will eventually establish a good habit.

2. *Sing*—in the shower, in the car, while you're getting dressed in the morning, while you're mowing the lawn, while you're doing the dishes, wherever. Dr. James says we don't sing because we're happy; we're happy because we sing. The *action* creates the *attitude*. It's a choice we make. Drs. Minirth and Meier in their book *Happiness Is*

a Choice say that we make choices in life—choices to be angry, choices to wallow in self-pity, choices to be happy. We decide which road we want to take.

For example, you may be extremely angry with your spouse, arguing and shouting, when the telephone rings. You walk over and answer the phone by saying in a quiet, sweet, kind voice, "Hello." Seconds after a shouting match comes calm and politeness. Why? Because a choice is made—a choice that controls your emotions. We *can* help it when we're angry. We *can* make decisions to do something about our attitudes.

3. *Read something inspirational.* Set aside ten or fifteen minutes each morning to read or listen to an inspirational message. That in itself can change your daily attitude. That in itself can give you confidence and hope you never had before.

4. *Associate with positive people.* Nothing can bring down a person's mood or attitude more quickly than someone who gripes and complains all the time. By associating with confident, hopeful people who are encouraging, your own attitude will be reinforced.

5. *Stop feeling sorry for yourself.* Most people don't care about your troubles and the rest are glad you have them! You can eliminate self-pity by counting what you have instead of what you've lost.

Fanny Crosby is known as one of the greatest hymn writers of all time. Born totally blind, she lived to the age of ninety-five without once having seen the light of day. But at the tender age of eight she penned the following poem which reflects Fanny Crosby's determination to make the best of her circumstances.

> O, what a happy child am I
> Although I cannot see,
> For I am determined in this world
> That happy I shall be
> For the blessings I enjoy
> That other people don't.
> To weep inside because I'm blind,
> I cannot . . . and I won't!

When people come to a point in their lives when they want to feel sorry for themselves, when they want to weep inside because they're blind, because they're unemployed, because they're divorced, because they didn't get a promotion, they must say, "I cannot . . . and I won't." It's a conscious decision to be made. We have the choice either to walk around feeling sorry for ourselves or to put the past behind us and get on with our lives and make use of what we have.

6. *Set goals for your life.*[3] Former light heavyweight champion of the world, Archie Moore, grew up in a crowded, hot, poverty-stricken ghetto. But he didn't let that stand as an excuse for not accomplishing anything in life. His ghetto produced not only Archie Moore, but also Clark Terry, a world-famous jazz musician, as well as doctors, lawyers, and many others who went on to make something of their lives.

"We made it," said Moore, "because we had goals and we were willing to work for them. The world owes no one—black or white—a living."

People can always find excuses for failing. They can always find someone or something to blame their losses on. But when it comes down to the final line in the story of a person's life, the last accountability lies with self. This is expressed extremely well in the following poem by an unknown author.

When you get what you want in your struggle for self,
And the world makes you king for a day;
Then go to the mirror and look at yourself,
And see what that guy has to say.

For it isn't your father, or mother, or wife,
Whose judgment upon you must pass.
The fellow whose verdict counts most in your life
Is the guy staring back from the glass.

He's the fellow to please, never mind all the rest,
For he's with you clear up to the end.
And you've passed your most dangerous, difficult test
If the guy in the glass is your friend.

You may be like Jack Horner and "chisel" a plum,
And think you're a wonderful guy;
But the man in the glass says you're only a bum
If you can't look him straight in the eye.

You can fool the whole world down the pathway of years,
And get pats on the back as you pass.
But your final reward will be heartaches and tears
If you've cheated the guy in the glass.

Make a decision today to do something about the rest of your life. Set goals to work toward.

7. *Be the very best at what you do.* Ninety percent of what you know about your job, you either learned in college or within the first six months of your employment. If you know most of what is needed to get the job done and still don't do a good job, whose fault is it? Make a concentrated effort to go the extra mile. Keep up in your given field. Make it your business to learn new ways to do your job in order to cut costs, time, and so forth. Force yourself into a habit of dedication and commitment that will pay big dividends in the future. Second Timothy 2:15 says, "... *Be a good workman, one who does not need to be ashamed when God examines your work*" (TLB). Be the very best at what you do.

8. *Don't give in to fear.* As noted earlier in this chapter, fear can be a most destructive force. You mustn't allow it to control your life. When you find yourself in fearful situations or circumstances, you must look around to find something you can do to make the situation better. You must remain in control. Succumbing to fear can cripple a person forever, robbing him or her of potential successes, achievements, and victories in life.

Singer Marian Anderson went to Philadelphia years ago to sing on the steps of Constitution Hall. The Daughters of the American Revolution decided that the building shouldn't be made available to a black singer. Protests poured in from all over America. But Marian Anderson didn't let this shake her faith. She didn't allow the outcries of prejudiced people to fill her heart with fear. She didn't give up and quit.

Instead, she took everything in stride and simply moved her performance. She went to Washington, D.C., where she sang on the steps of the Lincoln Memorial to over seventy-five thousand people. It was one of the largest gatherings in the history of the nation's capital. If she had sung at Constitution Hall, she would have probably sung to a maximum of three thousand people. By not allowing fear to grip her heart, Marian Anderson multiplied her popularity. Her "trouble" was simply a prelude to victory.

History would have been greatly rewritten had people succumbed to fear instead of persevering with an expectation of success.

• Winston Churchill failed in prep school and went on to flunk again in college. Yet he refused to give up and persevered until he became one of the world's greatest leaders in his senior years.

• Although he loved music, Irving Berlin never learned to play the piano. But by composing in one key and playing by ear, he became one of America's most prolific and famous songwriters.

• Mark Twain's life was marked by poverty. Yet he maintained his faith and became one of this nation's most prolific novelists and best loved humorists.

• Admiral Byrd spent years in oppressive loneliness. But he refused to allow fear to overcome him and eventually became an acclaimed explorer.

• Louis Pasteur didn't discover the revolutionary process of pasteurization until *after* he suffered a paralyzing stroke.

• Every year at Christmas we hear the beautiful words and music of George Frederick Handel's immortal *Messiah*. Yet Handel wrote the most encouraging words in the world at his lowest point in life—when he was paralyzed, destitute, and threatened with debtor's prison.

• Admiral Horatio Nelson who served in the British Royal Navy was often touted for his moral and physical courage as well as his enthusiasm and superior leadership qualities. On Valentine's Day in 1797 he lost an eye during an amphibious operation in Corsica. Five months later he lost his right arm in a skirmish in the Canary Islands. Undaunted by his losses, the admiral continued to serve the crown.

In 1803 the crown gave Nelson a command in the Mediterranean where it was feared Napoleon's forces were departing for a possible attack on England. Nelson blockaded the French for two years. At one point when his fleet abandoned him in fear, he hoisted six flags on the ship saying, "If five of the flags are shot down, I don't want anyone to think I've surrendered!"

Admiral Nelson never gave up. When the French escaped the blockade, Nelson chased them to the West Indies and back across the Atlantic to Europe where the French admiral took refuge and Napoleon had to abandon his plans for invading England. Nelson knew that he couldn't let his fears overtake him. Unfortunately, others have not been able to master that belief.

• In the fifties and sixties, Karl Wallenda and his family became the most famous tightwire walkers in the world. Their pyramids of from six to ten people on a wire forty to fifty feet in the air stunned audiences around the globe. Even after a major fall in which several of his family members were killed or critically injured, the senior Wallenda continued his seemingly fearless feats. Many times he would stretch a wire from one building roof to another, battling unpredictable winds and other elements of nature in order to perform for people of all nationalities. Finally, in 1968, Karl Wallenda fell to his death from a seventy-five-foot wire stretched over a street in San Juan, Puerto Rico.

Wallenda's wife, also an aerialist, later told reporters that Karl had worried about falling for three months prior to the walk. She said it was the first time he'd ever thought about falling, and that it seemed to her he put all his energy into *not falling* rather than *walking* the highwire. He allowed his fear to consume him to the point that it took his life.

I am well aware that people go through some very tough and difficult times. Maybe you're feeling low right now. But are you as low as Jonah when he lay in the belly of a whale at the bottom of the sea for three days? Are you as sick and desperate as Job who lost all his possessions, including his family, and then became covered with boils from head to foot? Are you as wronged as David whose wife cursed him, son betrayed him, and friends wanted to stone him?

No matter what your situation, you must *believe* it will get better. Until you believe that, you won't be able to develop an attitude that expects to succeed, an attitude that expects the best in life—even if the best has to rise out of the ashes of the worst. What you believe *does* make a difference.

Two travelers on a lonely road spent the night in an abandoned farmhouse. They were very tired and found an old rusting bed covered with a lumpy mattress in an upstairs bedroom.

"I can't sleep without fresh air. Open the window," the first man said.

The second man tried to open the window, but it was stuck.

"I just can't sleep without fresh air," the first man said, "so break the window."

The second man took his shoe and broke the glass. This satisfied the first man who could now feel the fresh air. So the two men lay down and slept like babies.

The next morning when streams of sunlight filled the room, the two men looked at the window and realized that the glass hadn't been broken at all. Instead, the glass in the door of an old broken-down bookcase next to the window lay shattered all over the floor. No fresh air had come in at all. But because the first man *believed* there was fresh air, he was able to sleep comfortably. What he believed made all the difference.

You must believe that times will get better. You must believe there is a purpose for your trials. You must believe you can learn from them and grow because of them. The next time you feel low, discouraged, and defeated, write down on a piece of paper the thing you fear most. Go outside and hold that paper up toward the sky. Look at the paper and the problem written on it. Then look at the vastness of God's universe and His awesome power and ask yourself, "Which is bigger, my problem or God?" Nothing is too great for God to handle. Know that He is bigger than any problem you may have.

I have carried the following poem in my wallet for many years. When I need hope and encouragement, I pull it out and read it. I give it to my clients so they may draw encouragement from it as well. Make a copy of it and carry it with you. When your day gets bad, take it out and read it. When the day is good, take it out and read it. I hope it will give you the hope it has given me over the years.

> Though everything is dark and drear,
>   I shall succeed.
> Though failure's voice speaks in my ear,
>   I shall succeed.
> I do not fear misfortune's blow,
> I tower with strength above each foe,
> I stand erect because I know,
>   I shall succeed.
>
> Night swoops down with darkest wings,
>   But I shall succeed.
> I see the stars that darkness brings,
>   But I shall succeed.
> No force on earth can make me cower,
> Because each moment and each hour
> I still affirm with strength and power,
>   I shall succeed.
>   —Author unknown

Set goals for your life, commit to a purpose, resolve to be dedicated to your work and your family, make a *choice* to be enthusiastic and positive, maintaining an attitude that *expects* to succeed. You must *believe* in yourself and in your God-given talents that whatever comes your way, you will survive it and overcome it. *It's always too soon to quit!*

7

Know How to Get Along With Others

One Saturday night, as the sun sank low in the sky and people began making their way home, a young grocery clerk locked the doors to his store and began to wrap up his day's work so he, too, could go home to his family. Suddenly, he heard a sharp knock at the door. The clerk walked to the front of the store to find an old lady standing on the sidewalk rapping desperately on the store's glass door.

"We're closed," the clerk shouted.

"Let me in," the lady responded as she continued to knock on the glass.

Reluctantly the clerk opened the door and let the old lady in. "How can I help you?" he asked.

"I need a head of lettuce," she said as she brushed past him and headed for the produce section.

The clerk followed her and watched as she picked up one lettuce head after another, carefully turning each one over and over, feeling for firmness, and weighing it in her small hand.

After about five minutes of concentrated deliberation, she said, "Well, the truth is, I need only *half* a head of lettuce."

This poor tired grocery clerk had worked a very long day and wanted to go home; this interruption had only delayed him. So, when he heard her announcement he grew very angry. He couldn't believe that he'd opened the store for this person who wanted only half a head of lettuce. But, being a sensitive man, he didn't want his customer to see his anger. So he explained that he must first get permission from the store manager before he could sell her half a head of lettuce. Leaving the old lady standing in the produce section, he proceeded to the manager's office at the back of the store.

"You won't believe this," he said to the store manager, "but some stupid, idiotic, cranky old woman wants half a head of lettuce!"

About that time he glanced over his shoulder and saw that the old lady had followed him all the way back to the manager's office and was standing there listening to him.

He slowly turned back to the manager and said, "But, fortunately, we have another lady here who will take the other half."

This young man knew how to get along with people. He knew how to interact and communicate with others in order to get positive results. Because he spared her feelings, he knew she would be back again as a customer of his store. The fifth characteristic of people who make their own breaks in life is they *know how to get along with others*. Not only will this skill help you get through tough times, but it will also help you *avoid* some of the potential difficulties described in chapter 2.

Knowing how to get along with others can have a wealth of positive results. It can improve relationships with family members resulting in improved marriages and better communication with children. It can enhance your chances for advancement on the job and improve business relations overall, gaining you new respect from your peers and supervisors. Knowing how to communicate can enable you to maintain good relationships among friends, preventing emotional isolation which is so damaging to a person's emotional well-being. Good friends provide a support system that, when tough times do happen to come along, will be an invaluable resource from which to draw.

Communication is defined by Webster as "a process by which information is exchanged between individuals through a common system of symbols, signs, or behavior." Experts tell us that over 70 percent of our waking hours is spent in some form of communication—writing, reading, speaking, or listening. Of the time spent in communicating, 75 percent is spent in just speaking and listening. With that much time spent in interacting with others, it's crucial that we do everything within our power to get along and avoid possible misunderstandings.

Barriers to Good Communication

1. *Bad information* is the first cause of miscommunication. Facts are distorted, inaccurate, incomplete, or too complicated to be understood. This is one of the more obvious causes of misunderstanding between people.

2. *Differences of viewpoint or background* may exist between people which can cause misunderstanding. No two people are alike and you should always be aware, if possible, of those differences. For example, social, cultural, geographical, educational, political, and age differences among people raise barriers to good effective communication. These differences also include language, religion, customs, dress, sex, occupation, education, traditions, and even hometown locations. Within families, differences may include age, likes and dislikes, birth order, personality type. It's important to know that these differences can cause two people to understand the same conversation or statement to mean two entirely different things.

Example: To a native Kentuckian *tank* means a tall metal structure built for the purpose of holding water. To a Texan, however, *tank* means a man-made body of water in the ground which is used for watering livestock and fishing. Now, every Kentuckian knows that's a *pond!*

3. *Interpersonal difficulties* can also hinder good communication. If any friction already exists between two parties, then miscommunication is almost a certainty. For

example, a young married couple who have had difficulty conceiving children may respond negatively to mother's comment, "When are you going to give me some grandchildren?" Or two employees who are angry with each other may have difficulty working together until that anger is resolved. When emotions are involved, people seldom even try to understand one another.

4. *Holding biases* may interfere with good communication. Certain words may excite attitudes and emotions which will motivate people *not* to hear and understand. These words are known as "red flag words" because each time a listener hears them a "red flag" goes up in his brain which tells him immediately that he doesn't like anything this person has to say. These words may be as simple as *democrat* or *republican*.

In addition, a person may believe in certain stereotypes. For example, she may think "all fat people are jolly," or, "all Texans act like J. R. Ewing," or, "all people who live in New York are rude," or, "all southerners are dumb." If you know a person has a particular bias, then that area of conversation should be avoided if at all possible in order to ensure good communication.

5. *Physical environment* can serve as a barrier to good communication as well. Background noise is a good example. Whether the noise comes from a television set, radio, stereo, or from children playing outside a window, the distraction may cause a person to become so preoccupied with it that he or she hears nothing else. Also, a room could be too hot or cold, or a chair could be very uncomfortable. Even a person's own physical state can become a hindrance. We all know it's much more difficult to concentrate when we're ill. All these things can interfere with the communication process and cause misunderstanding.

6. *Preoccupation* doesn't only occur with minor distractions present in the environment. Many times it is because we simply "leave the scene" mentally. A husband could be absorbed in his morning newspaper. A teenage girl at the dinner table may be daydreaming about her boyfriend. A child in a classroom could be daydreaming about Friday night's football game. School teachers know well how

disruptive classroom behavior becomes at the onset of "spring fever"—when attentions are turned out of doors and to the approaching summer vacation. Whatever the object of our attention, many arguments have resulted when preoccupation caused a person to nod in agreement when he really didn't hear the actual words spoken.

Many people become preoccupied because they're bored and their minds wander to more interesting things. Communications expert Ralph Nichols says that most people talk at a speed of about one hundred twenty-five words per minute and think easily at about four to six times that rate. Therefore, we normally have about five hundred words of thinking time to spare during every minute someone else talks to us. It's no wonder that our minds wander off to other things.

7. Some people have a tendency to *evaluate and prejudge,* deciding how they feel about the topic of conversation before all the facts are in. Assuming ahead of time how you feel about a subject or deciding that the subject is simply of no interest to you can result in complaints, accusations, confrontations, and putting one another down.

A husband may come home from a hard day's work and want to tell his wife about his day. She has decided that his job doesn't interest her so she listens with one ear and thinks about something else in the meantime. Or maybe a boss is briefing his people on a new project that's currently on the drawing boards. The individual who has no part in that project may not pay attention because the subject of conversation doesn't hold his or her interest.

Sometimes people feel their knowledge about a subject is superior to the speaker's. Therefore they have no more to learn on the topic. They assume ahead of time that their ability to solve a problem or deal with a topic of conversation is sufficient and they need no additional information. As a result, they don't listen constructively and may miss out on facts and details that could be important later on.

8. Probably one of the greatest problems in communicating occurs when a person spends the time that should be spent listening *thinking about what he or she is going to say* when the speaker stops talking. Sometimes it's possi-

ble to spot these people. On the surface they seem to be paying attention. They'll usually nod their heads while you're talking (sometimes known as the "woodpecker effect") or throw in a periodic "yes," "uh-uh," "Is that right?" or "I know." But all the while, they have a faraway look in their eyes and you somehow sense they're not with you. Their inattentiveness doesn't reflect on the conversation or the speaker. It's just that they're so concerned with formulating their own responses that they lose sight of the importance of listening to others.

With so many roadblocks to good communication, it's no wonder there are problems between people. It's a minor miracle that we ever get anything straight at all. If we're to learn how to communicate well with others in order to interact with them on a daily basis and in order to maintain lasting and loving relationships, we must first be able to recognize the danger signs—signs that communication is breaking down. Once we recognize the signs, we'll be more capable of doing something about the problem.

Signs of Communication Breakdown

1. *Misunderstandings develop.* Whether at home, at work, or among friends, if two people can't talk over a situation and explain their points of view and their feelings, then nothing except misunderstanding results. If we can't talk openly when we misunderstand another person's actions or motives or why he or she says certain things, then arguments and still more misunderstandings follow. Once this phase gets underway, we become suspicious of the other person's every word and action. We close our minds to their needs and motives and refuse to listen to what they have to say—further complicating the problem. Because of the suspicions that creep into our relationship, we stop communicating and wonder why the *other person* has changed.

2. Once misunderstandings develop, *frustration begins to build* because we don't understand one another and we begin placing blame. Negative feelings abound and we

lash out at the very people we love and need the most—without even knowing why. We just know something is wrong. Because of that frustration we shut out everything except that which interests us. We're jealous of our mate's activities and friends, although we've even shut out our own. We don't want to go anywhere or see anyone or do anything and we don't want anyone else to either. Everything makes us unhappy.

3. We become so frustrated from our situation that *anger erupts* on a daily basis. We become extremely short tempered, so fighting increases. We have no patience at all. We become so full of bitterness that we find ourselves saying and doing things to those we love that we would never have dreamed of under normal circumstances. We say and do things that hurt and cut to the bone and destroy all the trust we've managed to build over the years. I've seen husbands and wives say things to each other that literally destroyed their relationship. Even when one or both parties show remorse and apologize, it's never quite the same again. Nothing cuts as deeply or hurts as much as words said in anger and not out of love—words that cut to the very core of a person's being.

4. Finally, the *home or office begins to fill with tension* to the point that outsiders will notice. One person will usually develop an overbearing attitude—the "How dare you question me" attitude, the "I'm the boss and you'd better do what I say" attitude. This person never bothers to explain or answer questions, so communication becomes impossible. As a result, feelings of resentment occur. When that happens people begin manipulating each other. They want to be in control because their resentment is so strong. When the home reaches this point, the family and the marriage are breaking apart. When an organization or a business reaches this point, it's beginning to disintegrate as well.

Now before you become too alarmed, this is as normal as it can be. There are so many differences among people that no two will ever agree on everything all the time. People express themselves differently—some are quiet and shy while others are more openly expressive. People handle their feelings differently; some hold things inside and some cry or rant and rave. People make decisions differently—some want to discuss details at length and others simply say yes or no and go on to something else. People fight differently; some yell and scream, others like to dig up the past, and still others pout and turn on the silent treatment. The list is endless.

It's normal that we should differ. I believe God intended it that way. Wouldn't it be a difficult world if everyone wanted to be a leader and there were no followers, no workers? We must have differences. However, the important thing is that we learn how to handle those differences in a constructive, positive, and loving way without destroying relationships. Open, honest communication is the answer. Learning basic skills in nonverbal communication or body language, listening, and speaking, will help us to develop and maintain productive and lasting relationships. The small investment a person makes in learning how to communicate effectively with others will pay enormous dividends later on.

Nonverbal Communication or Body Language

You tell what you are by the friends you seek,
By the very manner in which you speak,
By the way you employ your leisure time,
By the use you make of dollar and dime.

You tell what you are by the things you wear,
By the spirit in which you burdens bear,
By the kind of things at which you laugh,
By the records you play on your phonograph.

You tell what you are by the way you walk,
By the things of which you delight to talk,
By the manner in which you bear defeat,
By so simple a thing as how you eat.

By the books you choose from the well-filled shelf;
In these ways and more, you tell on yourself.

This poem by an anonymous author illustrates how each of us communicates with others not only through words, but also through actions, behavior, and body language. Whether intentionally or not, we represent who and what we are in every aspect of our lives— through the clothes we wear, the words we speak, the habits we practice, and the places we frequent. Psychologists affirm that our body language usually reflects the inner person—mood, attitude, various emotions, and spirit. Everything we say and do is part of the communicating process.

Body language, or nonverbal communication, consists of all the nonverbal outward actions and expressions that contribute meaning to the spoken word, but which can also convey meaning on their own. They include facial expressions, gestures, eye contact, physical appearance, posture, various mannerisms, touch, and even how we use the space around us. The image we present to the world through these various forms of communication serves as a powerful example, so it's important that we understand more about the effect they have on our relationships as well as on our ability to effectively communicate and get along with others.

Communication experts report that over 55 percent of what we understand from an encounter results from what we *see* through nonverbal signals. Another 38 percent of what we understand comes from what we *hear*—tone of voice, vocal pauses, sarcasm, and so on. And only 7 percent comes from the actual spoken (verbal) message itself. Since tone of voice is considered nonverbal, 93 percent of our understanding of what others tell us comes from the nonverbal clues they give out. We judge first by what we see and *then* by what we hear. Why? Because the non-verbal clues are a reflection of the subconscious mind—a reflection of truth, of a person's inner spirit, of what he or she really feels.

It's ironic that nonverbal communication is the least talked about, least understood, and least written about form of communication. Since it has such a great impact

117

on our understanding and on our relationships, it's important that we learn more about it.

1. Gestures. Most people can't talk without using their hands because gestures serve as the punctuation marks of speech—they add meaning to a message and aid the listener in gaining understanding from it. When gestures supplement the spoken word, they become very effective tools in the communication process. However, some people have irritating mannerisms that don't add meaning to their words. Instead, these habits detract from the spoken message to the point where listeners find it difficult to concentrate on what's being said.

Johnny constantly jingles his keys in his pocket when talking to friends, while Martha either twists her hair or fidgets with her jewelry. Robert is always looking at his watch, although no one can figure out why. He never has anyplace to go. Jean plays with rubber bands, pencils, and paper clips when people drop by her office on business. Joe doodles on his memo pads when people come by to visit. None of these people can understand why others seldom remember what they tell them. Ask yourself if what you're *doing* adds meaning or distraction to what you're *saying*.

If you feel awkward unless you're doing something with your hands, use them to punctuate your spoken message with appropriate gestures, thus adding a liveliness to your conversation. If that doesn't come easy for you, simply place your hands in your pockets or fold them in your lap to keep them still. Try to become aware of other habits you may have that can detract from your message and then practice eliminating them each time you speak. If you want your friends, neighbors and co-workers to enjoy conversations with you and listen to what you have to say, their attention must be focused on what you're saying, not on what you're doing with your hands.

2. Facial expressions. When Laura told Bill that the Millers would be coming to dinner on Thursday night, his face fell as if she'd delivered very bad news. They'd been talking for several days about having the new neighbors over, and Bill assured Laura that nothing was wrong. But Laura knew better—his face had given him away. Finally, after persistent questioning by Laura, Bill admitted that a championship basketball game would be televised on Thursday night, and he'd been looking forward to watching it. Laura called the Millers and made arrangements to have them over on a different night.

Psychologists rank the face second only to speech as a means of communication. Facial expressions can reveal more than a thousand-word essay. They can show emotion as no words could ever show. The muscles in the face are capable of over 250,000 different combinations of expressions. You can show interest and sympathy or disinterest and boredom simply by a small change in the muscle positions of your face. Your mouth can show happiness, pain, sadness, and pure disgust. The list is endless. Nowhere is this demonstrated better than in silent films where the heroes and heroines had to depend on their facial expressions and body language to convey an entire story.

Be aware of the "look" on your face. Your facial expression should always coincide with what you're saying so your listener won't think you're mind is elsewhere or there's something wrong (you're angry, disinterested, bored, preoccupied, etc.). Show your listeners that you really are enthusiastic about them and your conversation together and that you really are concerned about their problems.

3. Eye contact. The eyes are truly the "windows of the soul." We can see in another's eyes a wide range of emotions and expressions: surprise, disbelief, love, hate, anger, interest, boredom, compassion, concentration, distraction, shame, grief, mischief, awe, happiness. Eye contact establishes trust and tells others that they have your interest and attention. And although it's absolutely untrue, we've been taught that we can trust people who will look us squarely in the eye. Professional con artists and chronic liars use this technique successfully on their victims in order to gain their trust.

It's very frustrating to talk to someone who avoids looking into your eyes. So, when you communicate with others, try to maintain eye contact to demonstrate that you care about them and have their best interests at heart. Maintain eye contact while listening to others as they speak to show that you also care about what *they* have to say. If this is difficult for you, simply look just above the eye or at the bridge of their nose. They won't know the difference.

4. Voice. The voice can reveal many emotions through the pitch, the intonation and stress placed on words, and the length and frequency of pauses placed at strategic intervals in speech. (Comedians use this "timing" technique to great advantage.) When the verbal message and the tone of voice contradict each other, people tend to believe the *nonverbal* message.

I've noticed that there is a correlation between emotion and the pitch of the voice. The more emotion present, the higher the voice. When you're angry, your voice goes up. When you're excited, your voice goes up. When you're terrified, your voice goes up. If I want to arouse excitement, I simply raise my voice. If I want to calm people down, I lower my voice, sometimes to a whisper. I've been told that you cannot carry on an argument in a soft, low voice. Try it! If you want to stop an argument, simply lower your voice. This is the voice tone where discussions, not fights, are held.

Moods can also be given away through the voice when they aren't readily apparent from any other source. For example, many of us have phoned a family member or friend and been able to tell by the voice tone of the person who answered that something was wrong. He or she didn't have to tell us verbally.

Sarcasm is apparent when the tone of voice and the spoken word don't coincide—when we say the opposite of what we mean. For example:

Father: "What's the matter, Jenny?"
Jenny: "Oh, **NOTHING!**"

Now, we know simply by the stress placed on the word *nothing* that *nothing* means **something.** Even though she said, "Nothing," Jenny wanted her father to know that there was definitely something wrong. Her sarcasm told him that much. She said the opposite of what she meant. Her tone of voice and spoken words didn't coincide.

When you're burdened by problems and your mind and heart are heavy, don't try to hide it and pretend there's nothing wrong. You can't hide these things from people. Your tone of voice and other body language will reflect what's inside and give you away. Remember, people gain 38 percent of a message through what they *hear*—not from words, but from the sounds in a person's voice.

To avoid being construed as insincere, simply tell people that you're having a bad day or you don't feel well. They would much rather know the truth than walk away from a conversation thinking you don't like them, are angry with them or have been insincere with them. This isn't the image you want to project. Any negative feelings you have will usually come through in your voice anyway, so you may as well explain them and avoid any possible misunderstanding.

5. Physical appearance.   Physical appearance is perhaps the most underestimated contributor to the communication process. People have a tendency to trust someone who dresses and grooms himself well more than they will trust a sloppily dressed person, no matter what his or her qualifications may be. Well-dressed people seem to convey an aura of self-confidence and authority that says, "I know what I'm doing and can be trusted and believed." That's why a number of large companies have a dress code for their employees who meet the public on a regular basis. And that's why certain religious groups send their lay missionaries door-to-door dressed in white shirts and ties.

In addition, studies of public elections have revealed that the tallest candidate usually wins the election because tall people seem to exude an aura of authority and competence because of their size. Presidential candidates have traditionally been advised not to choose a vice-presidential running mate who is taller than they are. President John F.

Kennedy was one of the few winning candidates who defied both odds by selecting a taller vice-presidential running mate and by defeating a taller opponent. But history has proved that his aura of self-confidence and authority and his refined speaking skills (including his body language) were major factors in his victory. The image he presented to the public was a very positive and confident one.

If we want to set a good example as well as build lasting friendships and relationships, we must care about how we look to others. We must take pride in our appearance and not look our best only on Sunday mornings. Take care of your physical appearance and your health so you will always look your very best when meeting other people.

6. Posture.   Just like the face and voice, the posture, or body attitude, also provides clues regarding inner feelings. We can rest our chins on our hands and look contemplative. We can place our arms behind our heads and look relaxed. We can place our hands on our hips and stand over our employees or our children, trying to look authoritative. We can fold our arms across our chest and look defiant. We can open our arms wide and reach out to invite a hug. We say a lot with our bodies, just as we do with our facial expressions and tone of voice. There are no better witnesses to this than the ballet, mime, and silent films. Where else are feelings conveyed more beautifully without words?

Body posture can establish security, confidence, and trust—or it can destroy all three. While talking and listening, don't fidget, pace, or look at your watch, intimating to your listener that you're bored with him or her. Don't stand over people, trying to appear authoritative. Sit *beside* them and look into their eyes on their eye level. Always be as considerate of others as you would have them be of you. By being aware of your body attitude, you can increase the chances of effective communication with those you meet and speak to. You can enhance your chances of presenting your true self.

7. *Touch.* We also communicate with one another nonverbally through touch. This doesn't mean just a hug now and then, although hugs are important. Touch applies to the business and social worlds as well as to the personal world. A touch on the arm, a handshake, or a literal pat on the back when someone has done a good job tells that person that you know he or she is important.

Years ago when my younger son, Craig, was about five, I took the family out to a nice restaurant for dinner. My three children were arguing that evening as siblings *always* do, but Craig seemed to be the instigator. My wife had just about lost her patience with him, and I was quickly losing mine. As we were reading the menus, Craig announced that he wanted a hamburger. We were in one of the fanciest restaurants in town and Craig wanted a hamburger.

"You'll not have a hamburger in this restaurant," I told him.

The two other children started kidding Craig because he wanted a hamburger and then World War III broke out. Craig was angry with his brother and sister and they were arguing with one another, and my wife wanted to crawl under the table. I told Craig he would behave or else, and he just sat there and fumed.

"I want a hamburger!" he exclaimed angrily.

"No, not here in this restaurant." I was as determined as Craig.

About that time the waitress approached our table. When he saw the waitress, Craig hunched down in his chair, his bottom lip protruding in defiance.

The waitress must have been watching our little family feud from a distance because she walked right up to Craig's chair, placed a hand on his shoulder, and said, "Honey, what do *you* want?"

Still defiant and headstrong, Craig answered, "I want a hamburger."

"All right," she said. "While everyone else looks at the menu, I'll go get you a quick little hamburger and then you can have something good to eat later on."

The minute the waitress walked away, Craig looked up at me with eyes full of excitement, love, and happiness again and said, "You know, Daddy, she thinks I'm *real!*"

The touch of a hand made all the difference. That caring, sensitive waitress taught me a valuable lesson that night. She singled out a little five-year-old and let him know he was important.

Touch your loved ones in some way every day. I know there comes a time when adolescents don't like to be hugged anymore. But as you pass them in the hall or walk by their chair, pat them on the back or rub their heads or pull their toes. It doesn't matter. Even though they don't like to admit it, they still need that personal contact and they need it *often*. Even though they're beginning to assert their independence, they still need to know they're important to you.

8. Space.   The way we use the space around us can tell others a lot about us. We all have what is known as our "personal distance"—that territory around us in which we feel comfortable. When someone violates that distance, we begin to back away. If you've ever met someone who seemed to stand right in your face and you felt uncomfortable and kept backing up, then you know what personal distance is. That person had invaded your comfort zone and you tried to back up until he stood outside it again.

Perhaps you've felt, as I have, that you must back into an opposite corner when several people get on an elevator with you. Everyone seeks their own personal distance and stays there until the elevator stops. It becomes uncomfortable when the elevator gets really crowded and people stand with eyes front staring at the floor indicator.

Personal distance varies with each individual. However, it usually measures from eighteen to forty-eight inches. It's the distance used for casual and personal conversation. Anything closer is considered to be "intimate distance" and is reserved for intimate relationships. "Social distance" measures from four to twelve feet and usually involves impersonal conversation. "Public distance" involves anything beyond twelve feet (speeches, assemblies, church services, public gatherings, school classrooms, etc.).

In addition to the varying distances, people behave differently when their "personal territory" is invaded. Personal territory is that space with specific boundaries such as a home, an office, a car, a desk, and so forth. I have a friend who used to teach various classes to employees in private industry. The classroom setup usually involved six-foot tables placed in a U-shape so the students could all see and interact with one another well. Two students occupied each table. When all the supplies and books were distributed, it became obvious where the personal territory boundaries were established. If Joe accidentally laid a book down over the invisible line, Larry would casually push it back.

Personal territory is also used to exert authority or status. The way we arrange our offices, for example, can either invite or discourage visitors. Physical barriers, such as large desks and tables, should be avoided when good communication is desired. Don't sit *behind* your desk to talk with an employee. Move around the desk and sit *beside* him. This one move will tell your employee that you care about him or her and that you're not trying to exert authority, but rather to communicate on a one-to-one basis.

This same principle applies in the home. When serious, honest, and open communication is needed, don't sit across a table from one another. Whether we realize it or not, there is even a position of authority at our dining room table. Why else does only one chair have arms? The head of the table is the authority position. This became quite evident at the Paris peace talks during the Vietnam War. When all the parties came together—the North Vietnamese, South Vietnamese, Americans, and other allies—it took weeks of haggling and negotiating before they finally decided upon the *shape* of the table. The North Vietnamese wanted to sit at the head of a rectangular table in the position of authority. Even a square table wasn't acceptable. They finally decided on a round table where everyone could be seated with equal authority.

When you need to openly and honestly communicate with someone, sit beside each other on a sofa or in chairs. Psychologists usually sit in a chair beside a patient because they know that this arrangement is conducive to open and honest communication.

Sigmund Freud knew the importance of body language when he said, "He that has eyes to see and ears to hear may convince himself that no mortal can keep a secret. If his lips are silent, he chatters with his fingertips; betrayal oozes out of him at every pore."

Be willing to show others through your body language—gestures, facial expressions, eye contact, tone of voice, physical appearance, body posture, touch, and your use of the space around you—that you care about what they have to say as much as you want them to care about what you have to say.

I have a good friend who owns a chain of small grocery stores in East Texas with a few stores in Arkansas and Louisiana. His grocery stores are the small-town type. He doesn't open on Sundays or stay open twenty-four hours a day. And he doesn't sell liquor or beer. A major grocery chain moved in and built stores right across the street from three of his largest establishments. He knew the competition would hurt. He would now have to compete with a "one-stop shopping, seven days a week, twenty-four hours a day" national chain. So he called me to come in and conduct some motivational seminars with his employees.

Several months after the seminars were held, all three of the competitor's stores closed down. The loyal customers of my friend's stores received service there that they didn't get elsewhere. His employees exuded a graciousness and a willingness to serve along with an enthusiasm that these customers couldn't find across the street.

Word about what happened slowly spread throughout the grocery industry. I soon received calls from about six different grocery chains across the country wanting me to train their employees in the same way I trained those in East Texas. One man called me from Mississippi and asked me if I could do the same thing for the employees of his 187 stores.

"Certainly," I replied.

"I have eighteen thousand employees," he said. "I'll pay whatever you ask if you'll train all of them."

This gentleman flew all the way from Mississippi to Austin, Texas, to discuss the plan and sign a contract with me. That particular day I only had about two hours in my office before I had to catch a plane to fly out for another seminar. But I set aside one of those hours for him so we could get all the details for the seminars ironed out.

When I fly from one engagement to another, I take along a small dictating machine so I can dictate answers to the letters I receive each week. Then, when I get back to the office, my secretary gets them all typed for my signature so I can sign them before I have to fly out again. On the day my friend flew in from Mississippi, I had a stack of letters that needed to be signed before I left two hours later.

We went into my office and I shut the door and we sat down to discuss the plans for training his eighteen thousand grocery store employees in Mississippi. As he talked about the pressure he was under, about the competition, and about his plans to try to get out from under his burden, I began to eye the week's worth of mail that needed to be signed stacked on the corner of my desk. So I decided I would just sign a few letters while we talked and in so doing I wouldn't fall behind on my mail. I could do two things at once. I could sign letters while I talked.

Seventeen minutes into the conversation, he stood up, shook my hand, said, "Thank you very much. I'll be in touch," and walked out the door. I was stunned.

A friend who drove him to the airport told me later that during the drive, he'd asked this gentleman what he thought of me.

"Oh, Lewis is great," he said. "But he's busier than God. He's too busy for me."

My reputation and my previous work testified that I could have done that job. I knew that I could have done that job. But my body language told him that my mail was more important than he was. I never heard from him again. I lost a huge account because I was too busy to give him all my attention and time. He judged me by my actions, not by my words. I hope that I learned a valuable lesson from that painful experience.

We must all be constantly aware that we have a

tremendous impact and influence on others through our daily example. That influence must be positive, reflecting the true inner spirit within us. Be very careful and aware of how you appear to others.

Listening

"You didn't hear a word I said!" Has a child, spouse, or colleague ever confronted you with this statement? It's difficult to communicate with someone who has tuned you out. Good relationships, whether they're between family members, friends, co-workers, or between you and God, strongly depend on good communication.[1] And good communication involves *both* speaking and listening because good communication is always two-way. If speaking and listening aren't present in a conversation, the results can be misunderstanding, confusion, frustration, and sometimes anger.

Hearing is easy. *Listening* is hard work. Dr. Ralph Nichols said that it is the most ridiculous thing in the world to be concerned with the Japanese "art of motivation." We could have solved many of our business problems years ago if we just learned how to listen. Dr. Nichols, after years of research and study, came to the conclusion that the number one way for me to convince you that you're important to me is simply for me to listen to what you have to say. *People don't care how much you know until they know how much you care.*

The question, "What kind of listeners are your parents?" posed to children on a communication survey reaped the following results: "They're good listeners when they aren't watching TV or reading the newspaper." "They're pretty good listeners when I'm talking about something *they're* interested in." These answers, while given by children, can be true of adults as well, and they reveal that our listening habits usually vary with the *reasons* we're listening.

If you invest your money to take a course at a local college, most likely you'll listen closely to every word in class because you don't want to waste the money you've invested in tuition and books. However, when you turn on a radio for casual entertainment while washing your car or cooking dinner, the radio program often becomes background noise to you. You may hear it, but you aren't really listening that closely to what's being aired. Unfortunately, there are also times when we become so preoccupied that even our family's conversations or discussions in business meetings become simply background noise. We tune out what people are saying, even though we've invested our very lives in our families and work.

One evening Joe and Carol were watching the evening news after a long and trying day on their respective jobs. Their three-year-old son sat on the sofa between them, chattering on as three-year-olds do. Both parents, absorbed by the news and their own occasional bits of conversation, tuned their son out. Suddenly, frustrated by not being heard, the small child reached up with his chubby little hands, took his mother's face, turned her head around toward him and said, "Hey, Mommy, I'm talking to you!"

There are certain things you can do to help sharpen your listening skills so you may communicate more effectively with your family and with others—things that will help you avoid problems that arise from miscommunication.

1. Pay attention, keep alert, and be observant. It's easy to become preoccupied and not hear what someone is saying to you. But, don't pretend you're listening. Sooner or later you'll probably get caught at it, and it can be embarrassing. You may nod your head and absentmindedly say yes to something you'd never ordinarily agree to!

If we can think four times faster than a person speaks, as Ralph Nichols reports, it's no wonder our minds wander while listening to others and we become such experts at tuning them out. It's also no wonder that our children and spouses often say, "But I tried to tell you so many times. You just never listened."

Being observant is as important as paying attention and keeping alert. For many years Frank and Martha worked for the same company, so they rode to and from work together, dropping their two daughters off at their grandmother's during the day. When the four of them rode home together in the evenings, the inevitable fight between the two girls took place in the backseat. This interrupted any conversation between Frank and Martha. It took them a while to realize that the girls simply felt left out. After a full day away from their parents they fought in order to get their parents to listen to *them*.

2. Use eye contact and acknowledgments. Using eye contact is one way of showing someone that he has your complete attention. And always try to look a person in the eye on his or her eye level. If you're speaking to a small child, kneel down and look at the child on her level. Don't tower over her. Believe me, you'll get better results.

When eye contact is inconvenient or impossible (on the telephone, for instance), at least acknowledge to the other person that you're listening. In addition, ask questions or paraphrase what they've said to clarify any unclear statements or just to ensure that you understand them. This technique also shows that you are truly interested in them.

Every morning, Mark sat at the breakfast table hidden behind his morning paper while his wife, Shirley, made breakfast. Shirley tried to talk to Mark, but he would only emit an occasional "ya" and "uh-uh." He never once lowered the paper to look at her or answer her questions. Shirley finally became frustrated and angry with her husband who acted out this ritual day after day.

"You're not listening to me!" she shouted.

Mark looked up from his newspaper and said, "Of course I am. It's my job!"

Many people assume that they're doing a good job of communicating when they're really only going through the motions. They hear, but they don't listen. I can't emphasize enough how important it is to *look at people* when they're talking to you.

It's much like the little boy swinging on his swing suspended from a giant oak tree in his backyard. Seeing his mother through the kitchen window, he shouted, "Look, Mamma, look!"

"Yes, I see," she said without even glancing in his direction.

"Look, Mamma," he shouted again. Only this time when he looked toward the window, his mother had vanished.

He only wanted his mother to turn and look at him. He wanted to know she cared enough for him to look out the window and take an interest in what he was doing. How many times have we done this to our children? How many times have we said, "Later, Johnny, I'm busy," or, "Not now, Mary, maybe later," or, "Yes, yes, I see," when we don't see at all? The most important thing you can do to improve communication with another person is simply acknowledge to him or her that you're listening.

The importance of using acknowledgments and questions can best be illustrated by an experiment conducted in a communications class of a major computer manufacturer. Two people were seated back-to-back on the floor and each was given a set of multi-colored, multi-shaped building blocks (not always identical sets). The instructor told one person to build something and to describe what he or she was building in the process. She then told the second person to listen carefully to the description and duplicate the project. The critical factor, however, was that the second person couldn't speak—not even to clarify instructions. Seldom were the projects even close to similar when this one-way communication took place.

The instructor then told the students to repeat the process with the second student now free to ask questions. This time, without fail, the projects were nearly identical. Two-way communication made the difference.

Effective listening is *active* listening. Simple acknowledgments of eye contact, verbal responses, and questions not only clarify the meaning of statements for you, the listener, but they also show others that you're involved in what they're saying to you, showing that you care.

3. Avoid irritating habits. Some habits may indicate that you're bored or not interested in what people have to say, even if you don't intend to convey that at all. It's important to recognize these habits and avoid them whenever possible. As mentioned earlier, such habits may include

- interrupting the speaker
- avoiding eye contact
- fidgeting or pacing
- changing the subject
- looking at your watch
- continuing to work when someone is speaking
- undermining the importance of what's being said
- tapping your foot or a pencil
- playing with rubber bands or paper clips
- doodling

Take a few minutes and think of some irritating habits that bother you when you're trying to talk to others. Remember that what others perceive plays an important part in a conversation, so also be aware of any bad habits you may have and practice eliminating them today.

4. Occasionally write something down. When listening to other people, take notes. This is especially important in the business world for two very significant reasons: (1) It will give the other person instant gratification because he or she will know you intend to take action and (2) it will assure that person that you won't forget what he or she tells you. When you write down what someone else has said, he knows instantly that you hear him, that you're paying attention, and that he has *all* of your attention. Assurance that something will be done is extremely important.

Michael came home from school and asked his mother for permission to go to a friend's house a mile away—farther than he'd ever been allowed to go before.

Michael's mother said, "Well, I'll have to talk to your father about it when he comes home."

She really intended to speak to her husband, but when he came in late he was in a bad mood, ate a quick supper, and went straight to bed. The next day Michael came home from school and asked the same question.

"I'm sorry, I couldn't speak to your father last night," his mother said. "I'll do it tonight."

The next night the mother was busy with a committee meeting, and the next night she simply forgot. The scene was repeated several nights in a row. Each time the mother told her son that she was sorry she forgot and that she'd do it that night. So Michael was continually put off and disappointed. After four or five days had gone by and his mother had not spoken to his father, Michael was faced with a decision. He could do one of two things: He could give up, stop asking, and forget it altogether. Or he could go without permission. Neither decision would be good for him or for his parents.

This scene could be played out at the office as well. Perhaps an employee would like to speak to her manager about a raise. The manager must clear it with higher management. But, because he failed to make a note, and because of his busy schedule, he forgot all about it. Two weeks later, the employee came back again. Her manager apologized and said he would do it that week. Again he forgot, and so on.

Forgetting is a cop-out. It takes only a few seconds to jot yourself a note and stick it on the refrigerator or put it on your bulletin board or calendar in your office. We're all very busy, whether at home, at school, or at work. Writing oneself notes is beneficial to both parties. You establish a good habit that helps you *remember,* and the other person knows that you care enough about him to be determined not to forget what he may need from you.

If you become known as a person who isn't reliable, pretty soon people will stop depending on you because their faith in you will be destroyed. I know you don't want that to happen. We all want to know that we're needed.

But we must work at helping others believe we're reliable and dependable, that we keep our word. Don't depend on your memory. Write things down when listening to other people, because *the longest memory is never as good as the shortest pencil!*

5. *Avoid the distraction of unnecessary noise.* The most obvious deterrents to good listening are loud noises such as the radio, stereo, TV, or a group of people talking outside an office door. The TV has unfortunately become a substitute for good family communication, and most experts agree that it has had an unfavorable influence on the quality of family life. Whether at home or at work, seek a quiet place for discussions where you won't have to worry about unnecessary noise.

6. *Avoid giving unsolicited advice and making automatic judgments.* Hear people out. Put yourself in their shoes. Remember what has been said about the difference in backgrounds among people—even among members of the same family. Each person sees things from his or her own perspective. Child number one, the firstborn and for a long time an only child and the center of attention, will view things differently than child number two, who was born into a ready-made family of three with a sibling already in the middle of it. Try to reserve judgment and advice until all the facts are in.

Assuming that what is being said is unimportant, or prejudging, must also be avoided. What is being said truly may be unimportant to you. However, it *is* important to the speaker or he wouldn't take the time to say it. A good way to hurt someone's self-esteem is to undermine, even unintentionally, what he or she has to say. This is done through criticism, ignoring the speaker, tuning people out, and making excuses of being too busy to listen.

7. *Don't interrupt.* This is so hard for me. Sometimes I get so excited that I can't wait to talk and I find myself interrupting other people. I know it's important for other people to have their say. They have a right to speak their mind and express their views. Even though someone may talk forever, the best thing to do is bite your tongue, bide your time, and be patient. Let him finish and don't interrupt. He'll appreciate you for it.

8. Don't finish what the other person is trying to say and don't answer questions or talk for other people. *For example:* Aunt Martha: "Jerry, my, how you've grown. What grade are you in now?"

Jerry's mother: "Oh, he's in the fourth grade now, Aunt Martha. Isn't he big for his age?"

In the meantime, Jerry sits on the sofa feeling left out and unimportant because he wasn't allowed to answer for himself. And we wonder why children, loved ones, or employees stop participating in conversations, stop talking, and stop communicating. Have enough respect for the other person to allow him to speak for himself. Children who aren't allowed to do this will grow up to be handicapped in their communicating skills and other more severe problems may result because of it.

9. Hold your temper. I think that when anger is turned on, the brain must automatically cut off. We say things out of anger that we would never say if we stopped to think about it first. Many hostile confrontations over the ages have proved this to be true—whether the confrontation occurred between nations, leaders, neighbors, or family members. People just don't think rationally when angry. Therefore, they can't make the best decisions nor communicate effectively with anyone.

Communication also breaks down when we provoke someone else to anger. This includes disciplining children in anger, reprimanding an employee in anger, confronting a spouse in anger. Try to calm down and cool off before taking action or communicating with someone with whom you're angry. Learn to control your temper.

Almost half the time we spend in communicating (45

percent) is spent listening. So, if we're going to spend so much time listening, it's a good idea to sharpen our listening skills in order to gain the most benefit from what we hear. Just as any other worthwhile task, it takes effort and self-discipline to become a good listener. But the results can be rewarding. Instead of, "You didn't hear a word I said!" wouldn't it be nice to hear, "Thank you for listening."

Speaking

Communication between people has changed greatly within the past two generations. Granted, we still use reading, writing, speaking, and listening to communicate with one another as people have done in generations past. However, with the advent of electronics, communication has slowly evolved from people-to-people to people-to-machine. Televisions, stereos, and computers have replaced people in the communication process. Not all of this is bad. Much of it is good. But when our children spend most of their time communicating with their machines, is it any wonder that they end up having difficulty relating to the rest of the family and to their peers? Or when a person spends eight hours a day on the job in front of a computer, is it any wonder that his or her communication skills have suffered in the process, causing problems with co-workers, friends, and spouses? People desperately need to practice their communicating skills in order to enhance their relationships and their chances for advancement on the job. In addition to learning how to communicate nonverbally and listen, they need to know how to effectively relate to others verbally.

1. Learn about your listener. Remember some of the major barriers to good communication are the differences that exist among people. So it pays to know something about the people with whom you communicate on a regular basis. And even though some of those people are family members, don't think you know everything there is to know about them. You'll be surprised what you learn simply by asking a few questions.

On the family level, ask questions often. Find out what's going on in your spouse's and children's lives—at school, with their friends, at work. On a social level, find out about your friends' interests, where they come from, their backgrounds, their politics, their religion, and so on, so you can understand them and relate to them more effectively. On a professional level, find out about the people you must deal with in your work. Find out about your company's origin, growth, philosophy, and goals for the future. Ask questions of and observe everyone. This knowledge will enable you to better communicate and get along with those around you, avoiding possible problems in the future.

Before making a speech to a new group of people, I often ask my host about the group. What is the theme of the meeting? What do you hope to accomplish? Why are these people here today? Are their spirits up or down? Are they feeling good about what they're doing? What are their needs? What do they need to hear from me? The answers to these questions enable me to tell a particular group what they *need* to hear in order for them to achieve their goals.

2. *Maintain eye contact.* Just as when listening, it's also important to look at the person to whom you're speaking. If he isn't looking at you, look at him anyway so when he does look up he'll see that you think he's important.

3. *Speak in terms your listener will understand.* This doesn't mean that you speak in one-syllable words. But, don't sound like you're reciting the dictionary, either. Don't hide behind fancy three-dollar words when you're trying to get a person to believe what you say. *Try to express, not impress.*

I once visited my dentist for a dental problem I had. After the examination, he tried to explain the problem to me. He used highly technical words I'd never heard before and went through a lengthy explanation of the problem and treatment—none of which I understood. It scared me to death. It sounded so terrible, I walked around for an entire day gripped by fear because I knew I'd probably lose all my teeth. The next evening I mentioned my experience to a friend who is also a dentist.

"Oh, Lewis," he said, "all that means is that you'll have to have a couple of teeth filled and then have some work done on your gums."

Why didn't my dentist tell me that in language I could understand rather than in his own highly technical terms? If he had used simpler language, I wouldn't have been frightened to the point that I almost went to a different dentist.

Glenn Kerfoot, a former communications manager for IBM, writes in his booklet, *Keep It Simple,* that communication

can have genuine strength and dignity and still be understandable. The Lord's Prayer has endured for centuries, though it was written in language a child can understand. Take a look at some of the great statements of history—phrases uttered in the heat of battle by men who wanted to communicate, not confuse. "Don't fire until you see the whites of their eyes," "Damn the torpedoes! Full speed ahead," "These are the times that try men's souls," . . . and that World War II classic of conciseness, "Sighted sub. Sank same." Clarity alone may not account for the enduring popularity of statements like "Don't give up the ship!" but it's doubtful that Lawrence's remark would be printed in every history book if he had said, "Please be advised to retain control of this vessel until further notice."[2]

The point is that we must say what we mean—simply and directly. We must be straightforward, keeping our language as simple and as human as possible. The most profound and meaningful statements are often short and simple. I can think of no better example than the words "Jesus wept" (John 11:35).

We must remember when we're communicating with our children, spouses, neighbors, friends, co-workers, bosses—whoever—that saying what we really mean simply and on our listener's level can save us time, energy, and perhaps grief, as well as promote better understanding among us all.

4. Always let the other person save face. I am firmly convinced that the greater the person, the more gracious the spirit. I think it's more important to get results than to come out ahead or "win" in a particular situation. It's more important that I keep my friends than it is for me to flaunt my ego or my strength by being always right. It's terribly important that the other person be allowed to save face—to walk away from a conversation or meeting without feeling like they've lost or they've been embarrassed or put down.

Most of us have had children bring home a bad report card or test papers with low grades. When questioned, the child may say, "It's all the teacher's fault. She just doesn't like me." Of course no child wants to admit he's responsible because in a child's mind this would be admitting there's something wrong with him. Children always want to look good to their parents so they'll be accepted and loved.

Our first reaction in a situation like this is to do the very thing that will erode a child's self-esteem—we attack the person instead of the problem by asking questions like "How could *you* make such a low grade? Didn't *you* listen in class? Didn't *you* study?" We point the finger at the child and not at the root of his or her problem. We do the very thing the child fears we will. The child then ends up feeling that he or she has failed the parents.

We can help our child save face in this situation by asking questions like, "Why do you think it's the teacher's fault? What exactly did she do to cause you to get a low grade?" or "What do you think you and *I* can do to improve your grades and change the teacher's opinion of you?" Can you see the difference? By focusing on the *problem* and not the person, we can build up our child's self-esteem, help him learn responsibility for his actions, and enable him to save face. That's much more important than pointing a finger and making accusations. Children must know that it's okay to make mistakes and, when they do, their parents will continue loving and supporting them just the same.

5. Learn to ask questions and paraphrase what others have told you. A study conducted at Oxford University revealed that a person can improve his or her communication skills by *400 percent* if he or she learns to ask questions. There are several reasons why asking questions enhances communication.

First, as long as you ask questions, you're able to *avoid arguments*. Two people can't argue when an honest straightforward question-and-answer exchange occurs.

I have a dear friend from Scottsdale, Arizona, who went home one evening after a long day's work, poured himself a drink, and sat down to relax and read the paper. He no sooner had settled into his easy chair when his young daughter ran into the room.

"Daddy, may I have a Coke before dinner?" she asked.

"Of course not, honey. You know a Coke will spoil your dinner."

"How come a Coke will spoil my dinner," she responded, "but a drink improves yours?"

This little girl probably didn't realize it, but her honest straightforward question avoided a possible argument with her father. After such a pointed question, how could her father argue with her?

Second, questions will *open the door for the other person to talk* because people usually love the opportunity to express their opinions.

My wife and I stood in line for forty-five minutes to see the film *The Return of the Jedi*. A gentleman stood in line ahead of us who was just as bored with waiting as we were. So, wanting to strike up a conversation, he turned to me and asked me if I thought the United States would ever place a man on Mars. Well, he asked my opinion, so I told him what I thought. I told him when I thought the flight would take place, how many people would be on it, how long it would take, when it would arrive, when it would get back, and even what kind of ship I thought would be used. When I finished, he stared at me for a moment in stunned disbelief, slowly turned back around, and didn't say another word.

"I can't believe you," my wife said. "You have no idea who's going to Mars."

"I know that," I answered. "But I knew more than he did, and now we're both happy!"

People love to give their opinions, and I'm no exception. We're all just waiting for someone to ask us a question.

Third, asking questions *allows you to maintain control of the conversation.* A good salesman will always ask a lot of questions. "Do you want your children to receive a good education? Would you like for them to have access to the most information possible for their term papers and research? Do you want them to be as prepared as possible for the tests they will need to take for college admissions requirements? Then you need this set of encyclopedias!"

I love my wife more than any other person on this earth. But, she has one little problem. She can't say no to a salesman. Sometimes I think there must be a sign in our yard that says, "If no one else is buying, stop here!" Of course, I've talked to her about this a lot, explaining how a person can say no to a salesman without feeling guilty.

One Saturday afternoon our doorbell rang. We weren't expecting company, so I figured some salesman had had a bad week and was coming to my house to get well!

"I'll handle this," I said to my wife. "Just watch the old pro. I'll show you how it's done."

A neatly dressed young man with a broad smile stood outside my door. He explained that he was a college student working his way through college selling magazine subscriptions. Then he asked if he could speak to Mr. Timberlake.

"I'm Lewis Timberlake."

"*THE* Lewis Timberlake?" he asked as he held out his hand to shake mine.

"Come in, son. Come right in."

One question from this young man changed my whole attitude. He knew how to melt my heart.

Finally, asking questions is the best way for you to *discover the other person's point of view,* feelings, needs, wants, whether or not they understand what you're saying. And the best way to make certain you've understood what they've told you is to paraphrase what they've said. Asking questions and paraphrasing are important psychological tools in one-on-one communication. This shows the other person that you're interested, that you want to understand, that you care, and that you want to hear what he or she has to say. This kind of communication can prevent disagreements, arguments, and misunderstandings that can lead to greater and more dangerous situations such as the breakup of a friendship or even a home.

6. *Turn questions into suggestions.* What I mean here is ask questions and then turn the answers to those questions into suggestions so the other person can come up with an idea to solve a problem or reach an alternate solution.

I had a friend who came to my seminar and told me he and his wife had problems disciplining their son. So he decided to take what he'd learned at my seminar and go home and apply it to see if it really worked. The next time he and his wife disagreed over discipline, he would ask her questions such as "How do you think we should handle this?" or "What is your reason for thinking that?" or "Why do you think that would work?"

There were times when she would be so angry with their son that she would suggest a punishment that her husband simply couldn't go along with. One such time the child had been so bad that the wife suggested what amounted to a short-term prison sentence. So the husband decided to apply what he'd learned and asked the same questions again, using her answers and his ideas to come up with suggestions and possible solutions.

"What you're saying," he said, "is that you want to ground him for six weeks and not allow him to go anywhere at anytime for any reason. In addition, you want to take away his TV set while he's confined to the house for six weeks with you. Is that what you really want to do?"

"Yes, that's what I want to do," she replied firmly.

"Did I also understand that you think an alternative might be that we only ground him for two weeks. Then during the weekends for the three weeks following he must carry out certain chores before he can go anywhere or have friends over. Is that what you're suggesting?"

"Yes, that's an alternative," she said.

"I think that's the best idea," the husband replied.

This wise husband and father had learned how to ask questions to determine the problem, discuss alternative solutions, and then turn alternatives into suggestions that on the surface appeared to be his wife's ideas. He had really combined both their ideas and presented them in such a way that no one "won" or "lost." He provided her a way to be in on the decision and a way for her to save face in front of her son. He managed to soothe the anger that had clouded her mind and prevented her from seeing things rationally and turned it around so that she was an integral part of the decision-making process.

When I heard from him later on, he told me that over the weeks and months that followed, their marriage and their relationship with their son became stronger and they all grew closer together as their communication skills improved. Communicating with one another openly and honestly without a desire to "win" can do wonders for an ailing relationship.

7. Learn to control the speed of your voice. A major butter company hired me to speak at a rally where they were going to motivate their people to go out and increase sales. When I got to the meeting, everyone was excited and elated. They had cheerleaders leading cheers and doing flips. They had a band playing upbeat music. These people were on an emotional and mental high before anyone even spoke.

Then they introduced the eighty-seven-year-old president of the company. He slowly made his way up the steps to the stage and then grasped the podium with all his might. He stood there for what seemed like five minutes looking at the crowd, and then in a slow, monotonous voice he said, "We're excited." As he continued his speech, the crowd died. They immediately lost the enthusiasm and excitement that had been so evident five minutes earlier. What happened? His low, monotonous voice dampened their enthusiasm.

Dr. Nichols says the reason most of us have trouble communicating is because we're *not interesting*. What we're saying and how we say it is boring to the listener. Therefore, it's our responsibility to make what we have to say interesting to others. One way to do that is to control the speed of your voice.

Most people think the slower they talk the better they will be understood. That's simply not true. In order to hold a listener's attention and interest, we must try to speak faster, not slower. Remember that we're capable of thinking four times faster than we can speak. So, the faster a person speaks, the less time his or her listener will have to become preoccupied. In addition, the listener will need to spend more time concentrating on what's being said and will therefore remember and understand more of the conversation.

I usually try to speak at about 220 words per minute with "gusts" of up to 280 words per minute, slowing down when I reach an important or dramatic point. By speaking this way, I hope to make the people who attend my seminars listen more attentively. But it's interesting that no matter how fast I talk, people will always be able to listen four to six times faster.

The Guinness Book of World Records reports that President John F. Kennedy spoke at a speed of approximately 371 words per minute during his 1961 inaugural address.

That's almost three times as fast as the average person speaks and 75 percent as fast as people think. Because his address created excitement, commitment, encouragement, and hope for the future, his listeners didn't notice the speed. Their concentration on his words made the speed irrelevant.

You, too, can maintain the interest of your listeners. By varying the speed of your voice, you not only keep from sounding monotonous, but you also force your listeners to give most of their "hearing time" to your words, thus increasing their concentration and understanding.

8. *The madder and louder the other person gets, the softer and slower you talk.* The voice serves as a weather vane for the emotions. The louder and higher it gets, the stronger the emotion. You can't argue and fight with someone when your voice is soft and low. That's the level for reason and rational discussion. Learn to keep your voice low and soft when the other person becomes angry. He can't argue with someone who won't argue back.

9. *Remove scratchy traits and habits.* The little clichés, slang expressions, and irritating habits we pick up in daily conversation can deter, detract, and diminish effective communication. *For example:* Whenever I see an average person interviewed on television, it seems that every other phrase is "ya know." Our parents' generation used the phrase "don't ya know" a lot. Perhaps we've subconsciously abbreviated a phrase that we've heard all our lives.

I once had an employee who constantly said, "Don't ya see." Many times this salesman would interview a prospective customer and he or she would take out a pen and make little hash marks on a note pad counting the times this salesman said, "Don't ya see." The customers were so busy counting that they never heard what the salesman had to say.

Whether your pet expression is "ya know" or "okay" or "I can't believe" or "don't ya see," you can get rid of it.

Tape the conversation at your dinner table and then play it back and listen to yourself. Or tape yourself conducting business in the office for a day. Believe me, nothing will draw attention to your speech habits more quickly than listening to yourself. You probably aren't even aware of how you sound.

10. Personalize your conversations. If you want others to be interested in what *you* have to say, use their names often—every third sentence or every 150 to 250 words. Ask them periodically what they think about the topic of conversation. By asking for their advice and opinions, you show that you're really interested in and respect their knowledge and opinions and any contributions they have to make. People who know they have a chance to contribute to a conversation and have a chance to respond will be more likely to listen to what you have to say.

In addition, begin some sentences with, "As you pointed out," "It's just as you say," "If I heard you correctly." This technique simply personalizes the conversation and lets people know you really want to understand clearly what they have to say, that you care about them, and that you're interested in them. This doesn't necessarily mean that you agree with them, because you're not saying, "You're right." You're merely telling them that you've heard their point of view. Psychologically, you've placed them in a position where they feel obligated to listen to your point of view as well.

Another way to personalize a conversation is to use the "me too" technique whenever possible. Say things like, "I'm that way, too," or, "I've always believed that," or, "That's happened to me before." People who can find a common ground can usually communicate more effectively.

11. Pause and think before you answer a question. Too many times someone will ask a question and we answer instantly only to find later that the answer wasn't well thought out. Perhaps we do this to show wisdom and strength and to show that we're always on top of things. But whatever the reason, we have to change that habit and learn to think for a while before answering. You don't need to take a long time; sometimes only a few seconds will do. But that careful deliberation indicates that you're thinking your answer through very carefully. Therefore, your answer won't be off the top of your head. It will be one that you honestly believe in and that your listener can believe in as well.

12. Be thankful.   Learn how to thank people for the things they do for you and be clear, specific, and sincere in doing it. Look in their eyes and call them by name.

For example: "Larry, that's an excellent report you wrote on the XYZ Project. I appreciate your thoroughness very much."

When possible, thank people in front of others. Somehow this has an added impact that lets them know your appreciation is sincere. Also, thank people when they least expect it—it will make their day and they won't forget you for it.

Most of these suggestions for better communication—whether they involve body language, listening, or speaking—are simply common courtesies. If we have respect for one another and practice the courtesies discussed in this chapter, our communicating skills will improve tremendously.

Several years ago one of this nation's leading retail stores put up a $187,000 grant to study a well-known life insurance salesman who made approximately $800,000 per year in commissions. This man was a phenomenon in the insurance industry. No one could understand how he did it. No one could figure out his secret.

After a full year of study, and after spending $187,000, the study committee concluded that his secret to making so much money was his use of the Law of Psychological Reciprocity. This simply means that if I give you credit for your intelligence, you are morally and psychologically bound to give me credit for mine. This salesman had only an eighth-grade education. But he spent his years as a salesman putting into practice knowledge that was much more important than anything he could learn in a classroom. He knew that if he treated his customers as the special people they were, they would respond to him in kind. The study committee didn't realize it, but they spent $187,000 to discover that the Golden Rule really works!

If everyone would use the "Law of Psychological Reciprocity" in all areas of his or her life, much could be done to break down the barriers to good effective communication. Tremendous inroads could be forged to enable people to get along better with one another.

Maintaining Relationships

Three hundred years before Christ, the Greek philosopher Theophrastus said that true friends visit us in prosperity only when invited, but in adversity they come without invitation. I believe that nowhere in history is this accurate view of friendship better demonstrated than in the friendship between Gale Sayers and Brian Piccolo.

Both running backs for the Chicago Bears football team, Gale and Brian began rooming together in 1967. This was a first for race relations in professional football as well as a first for both these men. Gale is black; Brian was white. But despite their color differences, these two athletes found common ground and enjoyed a lasting relationship both on and off the playing field. Their special friendship was later portrayed in the Emmy Award-winning film *Brian's Song*.

Their special friendship was put to the test two years later when cancer cut Brian Piccolo from his team—a severing experience that Gale Sayers shared because when one hurt, the other felt the pain as well. Shortly before Brian's cancer took his young life, the Professional Football Writers had chosen Gale to receive the George Halas Award for the most courageous player in professional football. Brian and Gale had originally planned to attend the dinner and ceremony together with their wives. But on that evening Brian lay dying in his hospital bed, alone but not forgotten.

When Gale rose to accept his award, hot tears stung his eyes as he remembered his friend whom he felt displayed much more courage than he.

"You flatter me by giving me this award," Gale said. "But, I must tell you that I accept it for Brian Piccolo, a man of great courage who should receive it instead. I love Brian, and I'd like you to love him. Tonight, when you get down on your knees, please ask God to love him, too."

No one wants conditional love that says, "If you love me, you'll do this for me." That's not love. That's selfish bribery and emotional blackmail that says, "I'll only love you under certain conditions." Instead, we need to express and invite unconditional love—love that is proved through one's actions—love that is consistent and at times even undeserved. That kind of love says, "I know what you are and I love you anyway—no matter what. I will always be here for you." To have that kind of love in a relationship, specific ingredients must be present.

1. Communication. We've dealt at length with communication. That is the basis for all relationships between people. Let this vital link break and it isn't long before a relationship begins to suffer. The easiest thing in the world to do is talk. People who've lost their arms and legs and the use of their bodies can still talk. But the most difficult thing to do is communicate—to open up honestly and reveal who we are inside. But that openness and honesty is essential to maintain lasting and loving relationships. We can't be afraid to show our true selves.

2. Authenticity. Being friends means we don't ever need to wear masks. We don't need to pretend to be something we are not, and we don't need to pretend that we don't hurt when we do. We can't be something we're not and still expect to remain close to people. They'll see right through us. And when we've been identified as phony, we'll lose the very people we need the most. Honesty and truth must flourish if we're to enjoy lasting relationships.

3. *Caring.* Communication and authenticity provide the basis for caring. We don't hide our hurts from our friends or our families because we know they really care. We sense within them a willingness to listen with compassion, not condemnation. And we sense when they're hurting and respond to their needs as well. We care about them as much as they care about us and our actions prove it.

4. *Acceptance.* True friends aren't on probation. Our friends aren't with us for a trial period so that when they do something we don't like we cast them out. People are either friends or they're not. Friends can disagree without being disagreeable. They can hold differing opinions without holding grudges. A true friend knows the real you (assets and liabilities alike) and accepts and loves you anyway just as we love our children in spite of their faults. We must accept our friends as they are—imperfections and all.

5. *Forgiveness.* Since we're all human, we're obviously going to make mistakes we regret. Friends and loved ones think the best of one another and refuse to linger over any offense. They're quick to forgive—and then forget that they had a reason to forgive!

6. *Involvement.* Friends and loved ones shoulder the same load, take on mutual projects, share one another's burdens and joys, and are available in time of adversity— even to the point of sacrifice. They let you know that any problems are shared. It's important for people to know they're not alone in the world. They need to know that their friends or relatives have had the same problems and can give them the love and support they need in their time of trouble.

The Candy Man

In 1857 a Mennonite couple in Pennsylvania became the parents of a son they named Milton. Milton lived a normal, happy childhood. When he was fifteen, he became an apprentice to a candy maker and four years later managed to open his own candy store. But the long hours of labor necessary to make a new business a success weakened Milton's health, and he was forced to close his business.

At twenty-six Milton moved to New York where he again sought employment in a candy store. This time he delivered the candy to his employer's customers in a horse and wagon. When the horse bolted and spilled all of his inventory, Milton again found himself out of work. So he moved back home to Lancaster, Pennsylvania.

Candy making was the only occupation that interested Milton, so he rented an abandoned factory and started making his own. Over a period of years he made first caramels and then turned to chocolate when new chocolate-making machinery became available. This machinery made it possible to mass produce a single item. So Milton turned his ambitions in that direction. In 1903, at age forty-six, Milton Hershey broke ground for his first chocolate factory. Within a few years he was a millionaire.

Most of the world has heard of Hershey candy bars. And unfortunately, that's what Milton Hershey is best known for. But there was another side to Hershey—a side that few people outside Pennsylvania know about. Milton Hershey not only built a chocolate factory, but also a town for the employees who worked there. He built houses for his employees along with churches, schools, stores, parks, hotels, a fire department, and a zoo. He lived his life by a lesson his parents had taught him at a very early age: *The surest road to success is to lose yourself in service to others.* Hershey always thought of others first.

Hershey and his wife loved children but were unable to have any of their own. So in 1910 they decided to open a school and refuge for boys. Here at his Hershey Industrial School, Hershey offered boys a chance to learn a trade. When each boy graduated, he was given a hundred dollars with which to begin his life and career.

Over the past seventy-five years, tens of thousands of boys have gotten their start in life because a loving, caring man lost himself in service to others. His generosity and love knew no bounds. When he died in 1945 at age eighty-eight, Hershey left most of his personal fortune to the school so children living after him could continue to find a purpose in life. The name of the school has since been changed to the Milton Hershey School and it now admits girls as well as boys. But its purpose and goals have remained the same over the years. It continues to this day to educate approximately twelve hundred students per year and serves as a lasting monument to a man who cared.

A statue of Milton Hershey with his arms around a small boy stands on the school grounds. The inscription at its base reads, "His deeds are his monument, his life is our inspiration."

All of our lives we've been influenced by the friends we've made and the people we've met. Much of what we've become can be credited to our friends and loved ones. We must treasure those friendships, and we must let the friends we have today know they're special to us, too. An unknown author expressed this sentiment in the following poem entitled "Touching Shoulders."

There's a comforting thought at the close of the day,
When I'm weary and lonely and sad,
That sort of grips hold of my poor old heart
And bids it be merry and glad.
It gets in my being and it drives out the blues,
And finally thrills through and through,
It is just a sweet memory that chants the refrain:
"I'm glad I touched shoulders with you!"

Did you know you were brave, did you know you
    were strong?
Did you know there was one leaning hard?
Did you know that I waited and listened and prayed,
And was cheered by your simplest word?
Did you know that I longed for that smile on your
    face,
For the sound of your voice ringing true?
Did you know I grew stronger and better because
I had merely touched shoulders with you?

I am glad that I live, that I battle and strive
For the place that I know I must fill;
I am thankful for sorrows; I'll meet with a grin
What fortune may send, good or ill.
I may not have wealth, I may not be great,
But I know I shall always be true,
For I have in life that courage you gave
When once I touched shoulders with you.

If you're to face adversity and the tough times life hands you, if you're to struggle to make your own breaks in life and become whatever you want to become, then you have to know you're not alone. The love and support that friends and family can give us are invaluable. They can never be measured. For some of us such a friend may be a spouse, for others a brother or a sister, and for some a good loving friend like Gale Sayers. But wherever that support may come from, the simple truth is we should grab on to it and cherish it with all our hearts and return it in kind.

Not only do we need support, but there are others who need our support as well. Each of us has either children, a spouse, friends, employees, or other loved ones counting on us for encouragement and looking to us for an example. We mustn't let them down.

In 1985 I was asked to judge an event in the Special Olympics. The children and young adults who compete in this program each year have been dealt a wicked blow that has resulted in either a mental or a physical disability. Never in my life have I witnessed more enthusiasm and dedication or more loving relationships than I witnessed on the field of Memorial Stadium at the University of Texas during this special event.

As I prepared to judge the last event, a motorized wheelchair race for paralyzed children, I learned that huge—six-eight—Kenneth Simms would be my judging partner. Kenneth played football at the University of Texas and went on to become an accomplished professional player. We surveyed the contestants and focused on a seventeen-year-old boy named Eddie.

At sixteen, Eddie, like all teenagers, had his whole life ahead of him and he looked forward to it with eager anticipation. At seventeen, a tragic automobile accident left Eddie completely paralyzed, unable to move anything in his body except his tongue. Moved by this young man's courage, Kenneth and I walked over to speak to him before the race.

"Mr. Timberlake," he said, "I heard you speak last year at Boys' State. You told me that God loves me and that I have a right to be a winner. I've watched Kenneth Simms play football and I've watched him win awards. Now it's my turn. I want to win the trophy today."

The race began and the effort put forth by those children remains unmatched by anything I've ever seen. Some of them, like Eddie, had to use their tongues to control and guide their electric wheelchairs. They rolled down their assigned lane, guiding the chairs around first one pylon and then another. Then the chairs rolled over a little footbridge and around another curve. As the chairs headed toward the finish line, I could see that Eddie held a comfortable lead.

The closer the chairs came to the finish line, the louder the crowd shouted. Eddie continued to lead and the crowd continued to shout. Then, when Eddie came within about six feet of the finish line, fear gripped his face, and he just quit. I don't know if his strength or his will gave out—or perhaps both. I stood there unable to believe my eyes. My body froze as still as Eddie's. My throat tightened, and my eyes burned as I fought to hold back the tears.

The crowd stopped shouting and a blanket of shocked silence fell over the stadium. Then, after what seemed like an eternity, a young girl in the crowd stood up and cried, "Don't stop, Eddie! I need you!"

When Eddie heard that girl's voice, a power surged through his still body as his faith and confidence returned. A look of determination flooded his face as he engaged the wheelchair again with his tongue. Once in gear again, the chair sped across the finish line to give Eddie a well-deserved victory.

The cheers and shouting of the crowd were deafening. Tears flowed everywhere. People were laughing and crying at the same time as they realized that Eddie had won much more than a race. Kenneth Simms picked up Eddie, wheelchair and all, and spun him around and around until he was breathless.

When Kenneth finally set Eddie down and managed to catch his breath, he knelt beside the wheelchair and took Eddie's hand. Then through a giant smile and flowing tears he said, "Eddie, if I ever play another game of football, it will be my way of saying I need you."

Someone needs you, too. Someone looks to you for hope and encouragement. Someone looks to you as a role model in life whether you know it or not.

Success may be defined in many ways depending upon one's standards and values. But the truly successful person—the truly rich person—is that person who is surrounded by friends and family. So it's essential that those special relationships not be jeopardized. By learning to listen to others with a sincere interest in them, by learning to recognize the signals of nonverbal communication and work through them, by learning to speak with people openly and honestly, you will not only enhance your opportunities in the workplace, but you will also ensure lasting and loving relationships. Knowing these skills will enable you to avoid problems that arise from misunderstandings and lack of support from family and friends.

When you learn to get along well with others, people will become drawn to you because you will have proved yourself a caring, capable, honest person. Their friendship and support will give you courage to face troubled times with renewed strength and optimism. And the loving looks in their eyes will enable you to persevere without giving up, because you will know *it's always too soon to quit!*

8

Seek the Source of Success

Here lies a man . . . name unknown,
Mourned in no one's prayers.
Where he's gone, no one knows,
And no one really cares.

Several years ago the Jaycees in a small west Texas town decided to reconstruct notorious Boot Hill as a tourist attraction. When construction workers began preparing the land outside of town, they uncovered the old cowboy cemetery and found a great many tombstones still intact. Workers cleaned it up and then the Jaycees held an opening ceremony so the townspeople could look over the tombstones and read the inscriptions that the old cowboys had written for themselves and for those they loved.

When I visited Boot Hill, I noticed that a small inconspicuous tombstone in the middle of the cemetery captured the most attention. I walked over to see what was so special about it. I have never forgotten what I saw. It bore no name or date, only the four simple lines above.

As I stood there staring at the cold, gray stone, all I could think of was how tragic that such words would be all that remained of someone's life. This man came to this earth and lived a certain number of years doing his best to achieve something for himself in order to leave something behind. All he left was a statement that no one had cared while he lived and no one cared that he was gone.

This poor man, like many of us, must have had a misguided interpretation of what success really is. Perhaps he never knew that there can be no dollar signs on tombstones. I sincerely believe that *a successful man or woman is simply a person who becomes all that he or she ever dreamed of becoming*. That really means that it isn't what you have but what you *are* that makes a difference.

All the wealth, power, and prestige that you can accumulate and enjoy in a lifetime will mean absolutely nothing when you're gone. Even one of the most powerful men in history knew that. Alexander the Great had conquered the world by the time he was thirty years old. But just before he died a few years later, he requested that holes be cut in his coffin so his arms could be extended outside. He wanted to be carried through the streets with arms outstretched and palms upward to show the world that even the most powerful man in the world left it empty-handed.

I recently came home from a speaking tour and found the following message on my answering machine:

Mr. Timberlake, you don't know me. We've never met, but I've heard you speak three times at my company. Each time you speak you end with, "God loves you, and so do I." The last time I heard you speak I was contemplating suicide. But when I left your seminar, I couldn't get that phrase out of my mind. So I decided to look for this God of yours—and I found Him! I am trying to live the kind of life I think He wants me to live and now I feel that I'm heading in the right direction. My marriage is stronger, and I feel better about my productivity at work. You don't have to return my call. I just wanted you to know and to say thank you.

What had I done? Not much. I had simply suggested the secret of real success is to seek the *source* of real success. I feel it's important for people to know where success really comes from. As I've traveled around the world, I've found that we live in a world of "almosts." People are "almost" happy. They "almost" have the car and home of their dreams. They "almost" enjoy their work. They "almost" have a good marriage. Henry David Thoreau said that most people lead lives of quiet desperation. I believe that people are desperate and frustrated because they haven't discovered the source of true success. I believe that far too many people miss the secret of life because they miss the source of life itself.

Life doesn't have to be meaningless, void, frightening, or empty. The source of life, as well as the source of success, is God. I don't believe the God I speak of is inactive, unattentive, or distant. Rather I speak of:

• A God so big that He created the universe and all that is in it.

• A God so concerned with detail that nothing escapes His vision or His concern.

• A God so personal that He knows the number of hairs on your head.

• A God so good that He can make servants out of your enemies.

• A God so concerned with you that He promises nothing will ever happen to you that you can't handle (1 Corinthians 10:13) and He will always be with you when the tough times come.

These promises can only be as good as the One who makes them. Let me point out that these promises are made by One who knows everything, never makes mistakes, and never thinks of anything but what is best for us.

I ask you not to close this book without reading this last chapter. I realize there are some readers who consider any mention of something as personal as one's view of God to be offensive. Further, I realize there are some readers who feel like they have "heard all of this before." Please don't close this book before you've had a chance to meet some of my friends and read their stories and before you can read why I believe what I do. Maybe it's possible that there is something in life you've missed—that there is more to life than you've experienced. But I want to assure you that there is a real and loving God who wants the best for you and the best from you. And I would like to tell you about Him.

The Wisest Man I Know

A man lived long ago who, according to published reports, was one of the wealthiest men who ever lived. This man possessed great power and was able to command and demand anything he wanted. He ruled over a greater portion of the world than any other man in history with, perhaps, the exception of Alexander the Great. History relates that he was obviously a handsome man because women were very attracted to him. He was also highly educated and people often sought his advice and learned from his wisdom. If you judged this man by the standards most of us tend to use, you would have to conclude that he was one of the most successful men who ever lived. He had it all: knowledge, wealth, power, prestige, position. He had what most people strive a lifetime for, yet read what he wrote:

> And I applied myself to search for understanding about everything in the universe. I discovered that the lot of man, which God has dealt to him, is not a happy one. It is all foolishness, chasing the wind. What is wrong cannot be righted; it is water over the dam; and there is no use thinking of what might have been. I said to myself, "Look, I am better educated than any of the kings before me in Jerusalem. I have greater wisdom and knowledge." So I worked hard to be wise instead of foolish—but now I realize that even this was like chasing the wind. For the more my wisdom, the more my grief; to increase knowledge only increases distress.[1]

Although a self-confessed believer and follower of God, it seemed the older this man got, the more disenchanted he became with people and with life itself. He obviously grieved over the inability of people to follow through with their promises and over their dishonesty. He finally reached a point where he questioned all of his beliefs. He wondered what his wealth, power, and prestige really counted for. Torn apart and his heart breaking, this man struggled with life and its apparent uselessness. Does this sound familiar? Does this sound like someone you know?

If you haven't guessed by now, this man was, of course, Solomon. The Bible says he was the wealthiest and wisest of all men—and I believe that has held true even to this day. Yet he came to a point where he felt that life may not be worth living—that it may cost too much to continue. But, let's read on:

> Well, one thing, at least, is good: it is for a man to eat well, drink a good glass of wine, accept his position in life, and enjoy his work whatever his job may be, for however long the Lord may let him live. And, of course, it is very good if a man has received wealth from the Lord, and the good health to enjoy it. To enjoy your work and to accept your lot in life—that is indeed a gift from God. The person who does that will not need to look back with sorrow on his past, for God gives him joy.
>
> Ecclesiastes 5:18–20 TLB

Solomon learned that wealth and power are wonderful things that we're free to enjoy because they're gifts from God. But he also learned a much more valuable lesson: A life apart from God is ultimately nothing more than "chasing the wind." Perhaps the reason I like Solomon so much is because I can relate to him and understand what he went through.

What Solomon Taught Me

I can remember when I wanted to be accepted more than anything else. I wanted so much to be popular and have all the things that money could buy. I wanted to be liked by the "right" people, invited to all the "right" parties, belong to all the "right" clubs, and so on. Yet no matter how many parties I attended, no matter how many clubs I joined, and no matter how many other accomplishments I realized, there never seemed to be any real satisfaction. I knew there had to be more to life. I just didn't know what the "more" was.

This feeling continued for a long time—long after I was married, had three children, and owned my own business. Then one day doctors told my wife and me that our ten-year-old son, Craig, would be blind within two weeks. There was no logical explanation for this tragedy. He hadn't been sick. Something just went wrong inside his little body and his optical nerve began to die. The doctors told us there are only 105 cases of this particular disorder recorded in medical history—and our son is one of them. We took him to other doctors, refusing to accept this unwelcome news. But everywhere we went, the answer was the same: There was no hope.

My perspective on life changed suddenly and drastically. I found myself in a position of wondering why I even tried. Like Solomon, I wondered if it was all useless. It seemed as though no matter how hard I tried or how much I struggled, the bottom always dropped out eventually. And I felt it had been that way all my life.

I recalled my earlier, more athletic, days when I occasionally got the breath knocked out of me. I wanted to get up off the ground. I wanted to move. But I couldn't—at least not until I caught my breath again. As I watched my little son slowly lose his eyesight, I felt that way again. I felt emotionally paralyzed, unable to "catch my breath." The money I had, the clubs I belonged to, the people I knew could not help. I felt helpless and without hope. During this time I searched for God and wondered where His goodness and mercy were—the same goodness and mercy that are supposed to "follow me all the days of my life." I needed help, and I felt God was off doing something for someone else.

If you read between the lines here, you will see that I thought I knew the aspects of God's character—those aspects *I* thought He should reveal to me. But God knew better. He waited patiently while I floundered in desperation and until I'd reached the point where I realized I could no longer handle the situation on my own. I finally stopped wondering where God was and stopped trying to control God and what I thought He should be doing for me. Instead, I began allowing God to control me, and I began making a concerted effort to live the way I thought He would want me to live. When I did that, I began to see other aspects of God's character that I had not seen before.

For example, God knows what we need to go through in order to prepare us for things we will encounter later in life (I learned this through hindsight). He also knows what we're capable of enduring. *He will never allow us to go through something beyond our endurance.* God has a plan for all of our lives and a *purpose* for everything that happens to us along the way to fulfilling that plan.

In 597 B.C. more than three thousand Jews were forced into slavery in Babylon. Jeremiah, the "weeping prophet," wrote, "For I know the thoughts that I think toward you, saith the Lord, thoughts of peace, and not of evil, to give you an expected end" (Jeremiah 29:11). That expected end is positive and good ("not of evil"). If we give God control of our lives, the tough times we encounter won't be eliminated forever. But they will eventually work out for our good. We must believe that they are a necessary part of God's ultimate plan for us.

Life didn't end for Craig when he lost his sight. He went on to graduate with honors from the University of Texas and is now attending graduate school. Through the experience with Craig, I've gained a great deal of compassion and concern for those people who have had to endure trials in their lives. I could have become a very bitter man and blamed God for taking my son's sight. Instead, God has made both Craig and me *better* men because of Craig's struggle.

Where were God's goodness and mercy? They were there all along. I wasn't able to see it then. To this day, I usually don't see it while I'm in the midst of a real problem. But it's there. And I usually find—again through hindsight—

that once I recognize the direction in which God is leading me or the purpose for which He's preparing me, then I can see His goodness and mercy more clearly than ever before. Most of the time we don't realize the purpose for our struggle until long after that struggle is over.

My son lost his sight. But I believe that every member of my family will tell you that we all became stronger because of a trying period in our lives when we had to trust in God. Our lives are better, our love is deeper, and our futures are more assured than ever before. We found a new source of strength, a new source of power, and a new source of life that has taken us through greater challenges and even more demanding times since. But we can approach those times knowing that there is a strength and a power to call upon and depend upon that will not fail us. God's promise in Psalms 91:15 confirms that: "He shall call upon me, and I will answer him: I will be with him in trouble; I will deliver him, and honour him."

Like Solomon, I learned that striving after wealth, power, prestige, and position doesn't bring rewards that last after I'm gone. Life is meant to be enjoyed, but it also has to be lived under the control of God. Solomon ultimately came to this conclusion as have many other great people.

God allows a person to be broken so that he or she can be made more beautiful. I am told that one of the most gorgeous places in all the world is the royal palace in Teheran. As you walk into the palace, you immediately think that the dome settings in the side walls are covered with diamonds. As you look more closely, you realize that the sparkle and glitter isn't coming from diamonds or even crystal, but from small pieces of mirror.

When the palace was under construction, the architect ordered mirrors from Paris to cover the entrance walls. When the mirrors arrived in Teheran, they were crushed to pieces. But, one of the builders suggested that the pieces be kept in hopes they could somehow be used. He even took the larger pieces and broke them up so all the pieces were of about equal size. Then he took the small broken bits of mirror and put them together, creating a beautiful sparkling mosaic. When a person looks at it, he sees an enormous distortion of reflections, sparkling with a rainbow of colors. It's an indescribable effect.

The mirror had to be broken to be made more beautiful. Isn't that what God does to us? We learn from the Bible that God allows us to go through tough times for many reasons. Perhaps we need to be tried so we may learn patience. Perhaps we need to be humbled so we may learn to look up to God. Perhaps we need to be weakened so we may know where our strength really comes from. Or perhaps we need to go through difficulties so we may grow spiritually in order that we might tell others what God has done in our lives. Whatever His reason, we must trust Him enough to believe that He wants only the very best for us. We must be willing to be broken in order to be made more beautiful, more whole, and more complete.

As the little boy led his sister up a mountain path, she began to complain about all the rocks in her way.

"Sure," her brother replied, "but the rocks are what you *need to climb on.*"

God can use our suffering experiences to help us grow—to help us climb to greater heights. We must look for the good in every situation (sometimes with twenty-twenty hindsight!). With God's help, we can overcome whatever life may hand us.

The Most Encouraging Man I Know

George Matheson lived in nineteenth-century Scotland. Everyone who knew him felt he was destined for greatness. An extremely talented and intelligent man, Matheson possessed an amazing amount of potential. He fell in love with a beautiful woman, and they soon became engaged to be married. Life for Matheson was exciting and full. He seemed to have it all.

Before his marriage, Matheson suddenly became ill. While hospitalized he discovered that he had an eye disease that would eventually leave him blind. After she received this news, Matheson's fiancée called off their engagement, leaving him with a broken heart. One day he'd been on top of the world; he had everything he'd ever wanted in life. The next day it all seemed to vanish like a puff of wind.

In that dark moment of despair when all his hopes and dreams were shattered, George Matheson could have given up and simply quit. But, fortunately, that was not his choice. Instead, George surrendered control of his life and its circumstances to God in a very unusual and moving way. He picked up a pen and wrote one of the most beloved hymns of all time, "O Love That Wilt Not Let Me Go."

> O Love that wilt not let me go,
> I rest my weary soul in thee;
> I give thee back the life I owe,
> That in thine ocean depths its flow
> May richer, fuller be.

Matheson knew that there was a higher purpose for his struggle. He recognized that his life could become "richer" and "fuller" because of it. His song speaks about the joy, power, and strength of God's love in times of trouble. But buried within that well-loved hymn is a third verse that speaks to the heart of suffering and trials in life.

> O Joy that seekest me through pain,
> I cannot close my heart to thee;
> I trace the rainbow thro' the rain,
> And feel the promise is not vain
> That morn shall tearless be.

That is the key—to trace the rainbow through the rain. No matter how bad things get, we must have the faith and courage to seek the rainbow, the promise of a greater, better, sweeter life.

The Most Surprised Man I Know

I heard a marvelous story several years ago that has made a marked impact on my life for two reasons. First, it makes sense. Even the hardest, coldest, most disbelieving person can see the logic in this story. Second, it offers reassurance. There is no more disheartening feeling in the world than the feeling we have when we think we're all alone and there is no hope. I would like to share this story and urge you to accept its simple, yet profound, truth.

A very successful man once lived in the city of Chicago. Not only was he an outstanding businessman, but he was also much more intelligent than many of the people in the surrounding community. As a successful intellect he found it very difficult to accept, understand, or believe the true Christmas story.

He was a very good man. He loved his wife and children. He supported the church in his community. He enjoyed his fellow man. He only had one problem: He just couldn't understand why God would come to earth as a Man, live a sinless life, subject Himself to temptation, suffer an excruciating death on the cross, lie buried in a tomb for three days, and then arise from the grave to provide salvation for mankind.

In this man's logic and way of thinking, he felt that an all-powerful, all-knowing, and all-wise God could have just snapped His fingers or waved His hand or spoken the appropriate words to save mankind. Why would He go to all the trouble described above to do the same thing? It just didn't make sense to him. The one thing he would not do was live as a hypocrite. He would not pretend to believe what he couldn't, so he continued to love his wife and children and support them when they went to church, but he couldn't go himself. . . .

People say it happened on a Christmas Eve. It was one of those special winter nights when the snow on the ground was two-feet deep. The snowflakes continued to fall, scattered by the bitter cold Chicago wind which whistled through barren trees as it blew off icy Lake Michigan. Our friend's wife and children begged him to accompany them to the Christmas Eve service to hear the Christmas story again, to sing a few beloved carols, and to feel that very special glow experienced only during the holy season. But the husband and father answered no. He just couldn't do it. They were to go ahead and he would wait for them at home.

He waited in the quiet comfort and warmth of his den, secure in the knowledge that he was materially successful, that he had money with which to provide for his family, that he had acceptance and prestige in his community, and that he had good friends and a wonderful family life. Life had been generous to him. Placing another log on the fire, he settled into his favorite easy chair to read, when suddenly he heard a thump on the glass doors that separated the interior warmth from the bitter cold outside.

When he looked out the window he discovered a small injured bird lying in the snow. Obviously attracted by the warmth and light radiating through the windows, the small bird had flown into the glass and now lay stunned on the cold ground below. He watched as the little bird tried to regain its balance, as it struggled in the deep snow, trying desperately to save itself from certain death. Being a good, caring person, the man realized that he couldn't let the bird die. So he stepped out into the cold night to pick it up and bring it into the warmth. He wanted to mend its wings so it could recuperate successfully and continue its life.

However, when the little bird saw the man approaching, it became frightened and began to flutter its injured wings, trying to escape. Each time the man inched closer to the bird it would flutter a little farther away, trying to fly but unable to, having only enough strength to stay out of his grasp. Each little hop, each little flutter of its wings, and the fear in its eyes worked together with the blowing snow and biting wind to captivate this man's heart.

The man grew colder and colder as he followed the bird around the snow-covered yard. Finally, exhausted and disgusted, he shouted at the frightened bird, "Oh, you stupid bird! Here I am trying to save you from the cold and from certain death and you won't even let me help you! Why are you so afraid of me?"

At the very moment the man spoke these words, the bitter icy wind stilled and distant church bells began to chime the familiar strains of "O Holy Night." As he stood in the stillness, listening to the bells and recalling the words of this beloved Christmas hymn, he realized the import of what he had just said and of what he had witnessed in his own backyard.

As the snowflakes continued to drift slowly and silently to the ground, the man fell to his knees and whispered, "Lord, please forgive me. How blind and foolish I've been."

Why do I call this man surprised? Just as the foolish frightened bird couldn't understand the giant of a man who had come to save him, so this man had not understood an unseen God who was trying desperately to reach out and save him, too—by coming to earth as a Man to offer undying proof of His love. Through the desperate fluttering of a small frightened bird trying to escape the unknown, this man came to understand the greatest love of all.

God is so great that He can become small if that's what it takes to reach you. God gave up His best—His Son—to give you the best, His love and power! You won't know the peace, love, comfort, and power available to you unless you take that first step of establishing a dialogue with God to learn what kind of life He wants you to lead. The final characteristic of people who learn to successfully grow through the tough times and make their own breaks in life is that they *seek out the source of true success*—the God who created you and me. What are your troubles? Divorce? Alcoholism? Drugs? Death of a loved one? Financial disaster? A child in trouble? Terminal illness? Loss of a job? None of these problems are too big for God to handle. God wants only the very best for you.

The Most Exciting People I Know

No one can tell more effectively how the power of God can work in one's life than the very people who have experienced it firsthand. Each of the following people has known real adversity. Some of them have shaken hands with death only to walk away and become stronger and more effective people. Their faith in God testifies to the love, peace, comfort, and power in the life of a person who seeks the source of true success. But their own words express better than I how that power has been their saving grace.

Sharon Echols' constant beaming smile and infectious laugh would seem to indicate that things couldn't be better in her life. Someone who doesn't know her well might think that her happiness derives from her husband's success, her home, and her family. Although these things certainly contribute to her happiness, close friends know that her inner joy comes from a power greater than anything on earth. Sharon tells her story best.

As a young woman my dreams were similar to those of most young women. They included a beautiful home, a husband, and children because I believed that most girls grew up to become wives and mothers. And I must confess that I was just a little bored with that dream. Little did I know what great pain God would allow me to endure to teach me what precious gifts a husband and children really are.

After we were married, Terry and I moved to Austin, Texas. During our early married years, God began to work in our lives to show us His plan for us. I learned two very important lessons in the years that followed. The first lesson I learned is that *God's love for me is unconditional.* I truly thought for years that the more I did to please God, the more He would love me. And I thought the less I did to please Him, the less He would love me. When I discovered through reading His Word that He would always love me unconditionally—no matter what I did—I began to fall in love with God. I then wanted to please Him out of gratefulness, not as a means to earn His love.

The second lesson I learned is that *God doesn't make mistakes with my life.* Terry and I had been married just two years when we discovered that I have an incurable systemic blood disease known in laymen's terms as lupus. With this disease, the body's immune system sometimes can't distinguish between foreign substances (bacteria, etc.) in the blood and the body's own cells. Therefore, the body attacks itself, often resulting in harmful damage to vital organs. My doctors told me they don't know how it's contracted nor how to cure it. All they can do is try to control it with medication. And the drug of choice is prednisone which causes its own long list of side effects in addition to those caused by the lupus.

The full impact of this disease didn't hit me right away. My doctors told me I was to avoid two things: the sun and pregnancy. Other than these two limitations, I had no other restrictions in my life at that time. So I decided that if I was to be a career woman and not a mother, I should go to college and get my degree. I had not taken college preparatory courses and the act of enrolling in the University of Texas was in itself a huge step of faith. But four years later I graduated with a degree in home economics.

During my senior year in college I learned that I was pregnant. I really thought I would be able to carry our baby. But my doctors gave me a sad prognosis that proved true when I miscarried. The full impact of my disease finally settled in on me. But so did the realization that I wanted a child very much. I had thought I would be able to deal with a childless marriage, but the pregnancy allowed me to experience the joy of creating a new life—if only for a few brief weeks. And I knew then that I wanted a child very, very much.

Shortly after I lost our baby, a special couple came into our lives. They told us how they had witnessed God doing great things in the lives of people who believed on Him for great things. I knew what I wanted to believe God for—I wanted a baby. A few months later, I learned that I was pregnant again. I was so excited because I had believed God for this baby and I knew He would allow me to carry it to term regardless of what the doctors had advised.

The following months were filled with a series of trials and tests along with miracles of encouragement. Nine months later our son Jason was born—whole and perfect and normal. The doctors were as excited as we were because they had witnessed a miracle. I had a child when all of medical science said I couldn't.

There is another side to this coin, however. I have been pregnant twice since that time and have lost both babies. The last pregnancy nearly cost me my life. This caused me to become confused to the point that I questioned what I understood about God's ways. I felt I must have done something wrong—I had not believed strongly enough. Several months after I lost our last child, a dear friend gave me a book that pulled back the curtain of confusion and settled my doubts. Through Edith Schaeffer's *Affliction* I learned that we are left on earth after we become Christians in order to bring glory to God.

One way we bring glory to God is by giving Him credit for answered prayer. Many times God says yes to a prayer and gives us what we ask for. Sometimes God's answer may be very basic and simple. At other times He may have to work a great miracle in order to answer our prayer—as He did when He gave us Jason. God is glorified through yes answers to prayer.

But God is also glorified when He tells us no. He had said no to three of my four pregnancies. During these times Terry and I had to trust God regardless of His answer. We had to believe that it would all work out for His glory and for our best interests—and it has. It is that trust of an all-wise, all-loving heavenly Father that brings joy into our daily lives—no matter what He allows to happen to us. This joy can't be expressed in earthly terms. It must be experienced to be understood. We weren't created by God to be able to have *real* victory in our lives apart from knowing Him. And the closer we grow toward Him, the more joy and victory we will experience.

For the next five years I enjoyed a relatively

healthy life. Previously, my lupus had been active only during pregnancy and had gone into remission afterwards. However, in recent years the lupus has become more active, coming out of remission although I haven't been pregnant. Throughout the necessary medical treatments and hospitalizations, God has taught me that complete wholeness in a person is a result of giving the Lord *all* the pieces of my life—even those parts I want to hold on to. He has been gracious in allowing me to live an active and full life in spite of the drawbacks, and I'm thankful to God for that.

I've asked the Lord to take control of my life and everything in it. He has done just that. That's one prayer He won't say no to. And I know that no matter what He allows to happen in the future, His grace, peace, and love will comfort me and see me through it because He is greater than any problem I may have.

Minister and author John Edmund Haggai says in his book *How to Win Over Worry* that most of our misery is left over from yesterday or borrowed from tomorrow. We must learn to live *today* through God's power for "He has taken back all your yesterdays (and) all your tomorrows are still in His keeping."[2] Mr. Haggai knows of what he speaks. The following excerpt from his book relates how relying on Christ brought him and his beautiful wife victory.[3]

The Lord graciously blessed us with a precious son. He was paralyzed and able to sit in his wheelchair only with the assistance of full-length body braces. One of the nation's most respected gynecologists and obstetricians brought him into the world. Tragically, this man—overcome by grief—sought to find the answer in a bourbon bottle rather than in a blessed Bible. Due to the doctor's intoxication at the time of delivery, he inexcusably bungled his responsibility. Several of the baby's bones were broken. His leg was pulled out at the growing center. Needless abuse—resulting in hemorrhaging of the brain—was inflicted upon the little fellow. (Let me pause long enough to say that this is no indictment upon doctors. I thank God for doctors. This man was a tragic exception. He was banned from practice in some hospitals and eventually committed suicide.)

During the first year of the little lad's life, eight doctors said he could not possibly survive. For the first two years of his life my wife had to feed him every three hours with a Brecht feeder. It took a half hour to prepare for the feeding and it took another half hour to clean up and put him back to bed. Not once during that time did she get out of the house for any diversion whatsoever. Never did she get more than two hours sleep at one time.

My wife, formerly Christine Barker of Bristol, Virginia, had once been acclaimed by some of the nation's leading musicians as one of the outstanding contemporary female vocalists in America. From the time she was thirteen she had been popular as a singer—and constantly in the public eye. Hers was the experience of receiving and rejecting some fancy offers with even fancier incomes to marry an aspiring Baptist pastor with no church!

Then, after five years of marriage, tragedy struck! The whole episode was so unnecessary . . . From a life of public service (my wife) was now marooned within the walls of our home. Her beautiful voice no longer enraptured public audiences with the story of Jesus, but was now silenced, or at best, muted to the subdued humming of lullabies. Had it not been for her spiritual maturity whereby she laid hold of the resources of God and lived one day at a time, this heart-rending experience would long since have caused an emotional breakdown.

John Edmund, Jr., our little son, lived more than twenty years. We rejoice that he committed his heart and life to Jesus Christ and gave evidence of a genuine concern for the things of the Lord. I attribute his commitment to Jesus Christ and his wonderful disposition to the sparkling radiance of an emotion-ally mature, Christ-centered mother who has mas-tered the discipline of living one day at a time. Never have I—nor has anyone else—heard a word of com-plaint from her. The people who know her concur that at thirty-five years of age and after having been subjected to more grief than many people twice her age, she possessed sparkle that would be the envy of any high school senior and the radiance and charm for which any debutante would gladly give a fortune.

Seize today. Live for today. Wring it dry of every opportunity. You have trouble? So do others. So did Paul who said, "Most gladly therefore will I rather glory in my infirmities, that the power of Christ may rest upon me" (2 Corinthians 12:9b).

Captain Allen Clark graduated from West Point in June of 1963 and three years later found himself on a plane bound for Vietnam. On Mother's Day in May 1967, Allen wrote home to his family that he had only eighty-seven days to go. His subsequent letters continued the countdown . . . sev-enty days to go, sixty-five days to go. In his book, *"Oh, God, I'm Dead,"* Allen relates the events that changed his life—events that occurred *one day* before he was scheduled to begin processing to go home to the States.[4]

The noose was tightening like a rope around our necks at Dak To. The other nine Green Beret camps in our area had been hit with mortar fire within the past few weeks, and we feared our turn would be next. I had time on my side. By June 17 I would be on my way back to Saigon. My replacement could handle this situation. . . .

On the evening of June 16 we could see activity across the Dak Poko River from our camp at Dak To. We were concerned, but we hoped for the best. Viet-nam, like all wars, was unpredictable. The dice were rolled every day, and we prayed—and sometimes cursed—that they would roll our way.

In the pre-dawn darkness of the next day I heard

mortar fire. But it sounded so familiar that I barely looked up from the letter I was writing to my wife, Jackie. The shouting of a Vietnamese man who worked in our camp put me on full alert. I pulled out my .38-caliber pistol and ducked behind a jeep. An American with a radio was on duty inside an underground bunker outside the mess hall. His super-secret special unit monitored the U.S. raiding parties in Laos. When I heard the firing, I called to him to radio for a plane to drop flares so we could see the enemy.

By that time the mortar rounds were hitting closer and soldiers were popping out of bunkers. I could smell smoke as I strapped on my M-16 rifle and grenades. Collaring a quarter-master corps soldier, I ordered him to one of our three mortar pits. Then I shouted to the men to put flares on the south wall where we had seen activity the previous night.

Confusion caused by the suddenness of the attack made communicating with the underground headquarters bunker difficult. When I peered over sandbags into the 4.2-inch mortar pit, Sergeant Cramer asked for a Beret to help him load. Rushing back to the center of camp, I found one sergeant and tried to grab other soldiers for the mortar pits while at the same time trying to spot enemy blasts so we could pinpoint return fire.

With a rifle in my left hand and a radio in my right, I peered across the river to spot the enemy when I felt a sudden thud which knocked me forward and I fell flat on my stomach. There is no flash with mortar fire. It makes impact and a splash of metal shoots out in a cone. One had hit right between my legs.

"Oh, my God, my legs, my legs. Help me!" I screamed. "Oh, God, I'm dead!"

Sergeant St. Lawrence heard my cries for help, ran over, squatted down and yelled, "I'll take care of you and get a litter."

Before he left me, Sergeant St. Lawrence grabbed a soldier and told him to take care of me until he returned, but the soldier ran for cover. Our men were firing, but the enemy's mortars fell ten to our one. I started to worry about getting a head wound, saw a nearby drainage ditch, and crawled toward it.

Sergeant St. Lawrence returned with Sergeant Cramer and together they placed me on a stretcher, still lying on my stomach. As the stretcher bearers slowed to make the 90-degree turn into Sergeant Hill's bunker, another mortar blast wounded both sergeants and my stretcher fell to the ground. Hill had been coming out of his bunker when two mortar explosions stunned him just before he heard my cries for help. After he got his breath, he helped carry my stretcher into his bunker. . . .

Sergeant Hill told me years later that when he checked my wounds he found that both my legs had been blown almost completely off just above boot-top level. He had run through enemy barrage to get morphine, plasma, and bandages at the Vietnamese first-aid station. He really thought I was dying because my face turned white as a sheet as I went into shock.

"I know I'm going to die," I told Hill. "I have no feeling in my legs."

"No, sir, you're not going to die," he replied. "You have a shrapnel wound in your leg and a piece of it is putting pressure on a nerve. That's stopped the bleeding, so don't worry about it". . . .

Apparently I never passed out in the bunker. I remember being carried out face down on my stretcher. The sky contained no clouds, allowing the sun to shine brightly. I could see holes in the tin roofs of all the camp buildings. Sandbags had been ripped open by the shelling, leaving dirt and sand scattered on the ground.

I couldn't believe this was happening to me. I had tried not to count on it—I had tried to just keep it at the back of my mind. But this was the day I should have flown out of Saigon for a week of R & R in either Australia or Thailand. After that, I would have returned to Dak To with my replacement and then headed home. My war would have been over. Now it was over, OK, but not the way I'd planned.

Shortly after 6:00 A.M. on June 17, 1967, two litter bearers laid my stretcher on the ground next to a jeep. Captain Gossett walked over and I told him that the medics would patch me up and I'd be back that afternoon. He said nothing. I really believed what I said. I still didn't know the truth.

Years later I would ask Sergeant Hill why I had not been killed.

"Captain Clark," he answered, "It was by the grace of God that you're still alive."

Allen was evacuated to the 18th Surgical Hospital at Pleiku in the Central Highlands of Vietnam where his left leg was surgically amputated four inches below the knee. His doctors made a valiant effort to save his right leg, also severely wounded. Allen was later moved to the United States Air Force Hospital at Clark AFB, Philippines, before he came home to be treated at Brooke Army General in San Antonio, Texas.

Allen's right leg continued to give him agonizing pain— pain so great that doctors found it necessary to anesthetize him before they could change his bandages. He required shots of Demerol every three hours, and even that wasn't enough to even come close to making him comfortable. His doctors told him that even if his right leg did heal, it would never function properly. But since the healing process didn't seem to be taking its course, doctors found it necessary to finally amputate his right leg three inches below the knee.

Recovering from two amputations proved to be a long and trying experience for this young army captain. He went through surgery two more times—once in October 1967 and again in February 1968. He had to build up his upper body strength as well as the weakened muscles in his thighs. And he had to learn to walk again with the aid of artificial legs. He took his first steps on October 5, 1968, while holding on to two parallel bars. With those first steps, his road back to a normal life now looked shorter.

After his recovery, Allen enrolled in the Graduate School of Business at Southern Methodist University in Dallas where he received a master's degree in business administration in June of 1970. In the fall of that same year he was awarded the medal of valor, the Silver Star. He would add this to the other medals he had earned in Vietnam—the Bronze Star, Purple Heart, Combat Infantryman's Badge, Air Medal, and Vietnam Service Medal with two battle stars.

Although Allen admits that God sustained him while in Vietnam and later in the hospitals, he says he didn't establish a personal relationship with God until after his ordeal. In 1972 he began attending church regularly with his wife and baby daughter. One Sunday his pastor preached a sermon in which he said, "The real war in the world is the war between good and evil, the devil versus the Lord, and they are fighting for the hearts and souls of people."

"It made me think," Allen says.[5]

Here I was a dedicated citizen and sincere patriot. I had almost given my life to fight the Communists, who in my mind were evil. I had also given time to the community and civic endeavors. I loved my country. I always had, but I had not given myself to the "ultimate provider"—God and His Son, Jesus Christ.

I shed a few tears in that service thinking that even though I had fought battles, the level where true battles are fought is the deep spiritual level. It was at that service that I became "born again,"—I knew and accepted John 3:16: *"For God so loved the world, that He gave His only begotten Son, that whosoever believeth in Him should not perish, but have everlasting life."*

. . . In my daily prayers, I thank God for saving me on the battlefield at Dak To. I feel that by His divine intervention the mortar round hit just the right place it did and caused just the wound it did so that I could continue on, have children, and make a contribution in life. I also get great satisfaction out of knowing that when I pray for forgiveness of my sins, the slate is wiped clean. Many times I've prayed for certain things and they have not come about. That means that I really didn't need them. The Lord provides *all* my needs.

Allen Clark realized after he came to know the Lord that God had been with him even when he didn't know it. He had nurtured and protected him throughout his life, including the time he fought on the battlefields of Vietnam. Even though he was terribly wounded and eventually lost both legs, his life had been protected. For example, one day while he was recovering in the hospital, a doctor walked into his room just in time to stop an air bubble from going through his IV into his bloodstream and to his heart. That would have meant certain death. And even though Allen suffered debilitating wounds, they weren't severe enough to prevent him and Jackie from having two beautiful daughters, Elizabeth and Christi, after his return from the war. As he said, the Lord provided *all* his needs.

I am honored to say that I personally know two of the three preceding people, and my life is stronger because of that. They have all felt despair, despondency, or depression and yet were also able to feel the loving hand of God on their shoulders—a hand that guided them through their darkest hours. It takes a courageous step of faith to give God control of all the pieces in your life.

Just as God allowed a test of Job's faith, so He allows trials and tribulations to come into our lives. Job was tested where it hurt most—the things that meant the most to Job were all destroyed. Job was a very prosperous family man who lived an upright and honest life and was greatly respected by his friends and peers. But Job lost everything: his wealth, his children, and his health. Finally, his wife and friends deserted him in his hour of greatest need.

I am thankful that most of us will never have to endure tough times to the extent that Job did. Simply reading the first few verses of Job 42 shows us how lonely and despondent he was. But there are two very important lessons we can learn from Job. First, God put a limit on the kinds of tests Job would face. God only allowed Job to be tested to the degree that Job could withstand it. Job could have quit anywhere along the line (and was urged to do so by his wife and friends), but he knew it was too soon to give up. When the testing was completed, Job had a wonderful perspective on God and himself that very few people ever reach in their lifetimes.

Second, throughout all this misfortune, Job remained steadfast in his faith. He refused to believe that God had deserted him as his wife and friends had. He continued to believe that a loving God can be trusted even in the direst of circumstances. Job was right. God never once deserted Job in his time of testing. And because of Job's faithfulness—because throughout his turmoil he continued to love and obey his Lord—God rewarded Job by returning all he had lost and more. Job 42:10 says that ". . . the Lord gave Job twice as much as he had before." He found new wealth and prosperity. He had more children and found new friends who would not desert him.

While most of us may not have experienced the total loss that Job experienced, many of us have been tested to *our own* limits and have lived through our own despair, despondency, depression, and deception. If Job could continue to seek God in the face of all of this, you can, too. I realize that it's an extremely difficult task to surrender one's life to God. It flies against every natural feeling in our body. But we can take our lead from Job and begin to learn how it's done. We can learn to surrender *everything* to God. Try the following exercise that can set you on the path of total surrender.

Write down the five things in life that mean the most to you—things you honestly believe you just cannot do without. Take your list and study it very, very carefully.

Now cross out the one thing on the list that you could

live without if you had to. This will leave you with four things that you feel you cannot do without in your life. This may be a difficult decision, but you must leave only four.

Review the list one more time in depth. Now cross out *one more item* that you could live without if you had to. This will leave you with three things that you feel are the most important things in life.

Study your list again and then cross out one more item, leaving the two most important things to you in the whole world.

Finally comes the hardest part. Cross out one more item of these last two that, if you had to live without it, you could. This one remaining thing should be the most important thing in life to you—the one thing you just cannot live without.

Look at this item very carefully. Think about it. Study it. If this is the one thing in life that you honestly believe you cannot live without, is there a chance you could lose it? If so, then you are doomed to live your life in insecurity! You are doomed to live your life knowing that the one most important thing in your life is a thing you cannot keep. This is the point Albert Schweitzer tried to make when he said, "If there is something in your life that you cannot do without, you do not own it, it owns you."

Another wise man, Jim Elliot, once said, "He is no fool to give that which he cannot keep in order to gain that which he cannot lose."

You cannot keep the material things of your life. But if you seek God, you can obtain an unmatchable gift. God's gift is one of love, not fear. He wants to provide love, peace, and power for you. Second Timothy 1:7 says, "For God hath not given us the spirit of fear; but of power, and of love, and of a sound mind." Proverbs 29:25 promises, "The fear of man bringeth a snare: but whoso putteth his trust in the Lord shall be safe." God loves each of us so much that His greatest joy is as our greatest joy!

Several years ago I spoke at the Hilton Hotel in Los Angeles. I arrived a few minutes late and rushed into the ballroom to discover that the meeting was running ahead of schedule. In order to fill the time between the previous speaker and myself, the host had introduced one of their own people to share his story for a few minutes. I was surprised to see the man they had chosen: a small, frail, and obviously frightened man. I sat at the back of the room and listened to his whispering, barely audible voice and wondered why they had picked him. His appearance was less than inspiring and I thought his story would be the same.

But as this little man began to speak, I saw an amazing transformation take place. In place of the weak, frail, frightened little man, a giant began to emerge. This was a man of conviction and character, a man whose words seemed to move the audience from apathy to excitement and assurance—a transformation difficult to describe and almost impossible to match.

He related that he'd been born on the wrong side of the tracks in a town too small to mention. His parents didn't want him and let him know it frequently. His life was miserable. But he grew up with one desire: to finish school and get out of that town as quickly as he could. He barely managed to get through school, but he did. And when he did, he promptly left town.

He arrived in a larger city, found a job, and enrolled in college part-time. He eventually obtained a degree in accounting and got an even better job. There, he met a woman who came from a similar background. She, too, had grown up feeling that she was less than nothing and not caring very much about herself or her life. Their similarities became the basis for a common bond that resulted in marriage.

Together, these two people found a strength within themselves that they had been unable to find at anytime previously. They joined a small church and soon experienced a personal encounter with a living, loving God. Their lives were transformed. They discovered that they no longer disliked who they were and where they'd come from. They now felt hope and joy and wanted to make a better life for themselves and for the baby they were expecting. They wanted to make certain, as we all do as parents, that their baby would have the opportunity to enjoy and experience life more than they had as children.

Their daughter grew and progressed in school. She took music lessons and joined the marching band in junior high school. As a senior, she played first trumpet in a band that was chosen to march during halftime at the Rose Bowl on New Year's Day. The proud parents stood in line for hours to purchase tickets for a football game that they had not come to watch. They were there for the halftime show. They were excited and proud to be in a stadium with thousands of people who would watch their daughter, the lead trumpet player, march onto the field and perform.

As the bands were introduced at halftime, this father and mother felt lumps in their throats and tears in their eyes as they experienced joy they had never felt before. They finally realized that their lives were not in vain. They had made life better for their daughter and for those she would bring into the world. God had given them a special gift that would outlast them and anything that they could do or accomplish on earth.

The bands marched onto the field to a cheering, exuberant crowd. Their daughter's band gave the best performance they'd ever given and basked in the applause and cheers of an appreciative audience. When it was over, the eyes of these two parents were glued to their daughter's face—a face radiant with excitement and joy. The father made his way through the crowd, down the bleachers, and to the sidelines where the bands stood waiting to file up to their seats. He grabbed his daughter and embraced her, wanting to share this moment of joy.

After a moment a teary-eyed father said, "Honey, tell me about it! How does it feel?"

"Oh, Daddy!" she cried. "You just can't know. It's the greatest feeling in the world. Daddy, there's no way anything in the world could ever match the experience I just had!"

The loving father held her for a moment and looked deep into her eyes, and with a choking voice managed to whisper, "Oh, yes, honey, there is. There is one thing that is more exciting and more enjoyable. There is one moment in life that surpasses even this. It is when *you* are sitting at the top of the stands, one of thousands of people cheering, and you know it's *your* child they're applauding."

God loves us as we love our own children. When one of us finds happiness, God experiences the same joy as we do when we see our own children succeed. That's the God I want you to seek out. The God who experiences the same elation as this father did for his daughter. The God whose heart swells with joy when one of His children finally finds the peace, love, and power promised in John 10:10: "I am come that they might have life, and that they might have it more abundantly."

Nothing is too big for God to handle—disease isn't, poverty isn't, divorce isn't, alcoholism isn't, drug abuse isn't, loss of a loved one isn't, depression isn't, despair isn't. In fact, God can handle all of them better than you can. He knows what it's like because He's been there, too. Hebrews 2:18 says, "Since [Jesus] himself has now been through suffering and temptation, he knows what it is like when we suffer and are tempted, and he is wonderfully able to help us" (TLB).

It's never too soon nor too late to put your trust in God. He will care for you through your trials and your fears. You will discover a new inner peace that will give you courage and hope.

> When things go wrong, as they sometimes will,
> When the road you're trudging seems all uphill,
> When the funds are low and the debts are high,
> And you want to smile, but you have to sigh;
> When care is pressing you down a bit,
> Rest! if you must—but never quit.
>
> Life is queer, with its twists and turns,
> As every one of us sometimes learns,
> And many a failure turns about
> When he might have won if he had stuck it out;
> Stick to your task, though the pace seems slow—
> You may succeed with one more blow.

Seek the Source of Success

Success is failure turned inside out—
The silver tint of the clouds of doubt—
And you never can tell how close you are,
It may be near when it seems afar;
So stick to the fight when you're hardest hit—
It's when things seem worse that YOU MUSTN'T QUIT.

As a matter of fact, *it's always too soon to quit!*

Afterword:

My Hope for Your Tomorrow

As you walk along life's path, it is my sincere hope that, no matter how many times you stumble and no matter how many obstacles you encounter, you will realize that *failure is never final* because the only time you fail is when you fail to try. It is my hope that you will find something in life that will fuel a

Burning desire within you that will capture your imagination, inflame your spirit, and energize your God-given talents and abilities. It is my hope that you will take on the spirit of

Reviresco that will enable you to persevere and flourish in adversity—a spirit and attitude that will allow you to see every obstacle in your path not as a stumbling block but as a stepping-stone. It is my hope that you will develop an

Enthusiasm for your goals in life that will wake you up in the morning and keep you going through the day so you will refuse to settle for second best and go after your dreams. May you have an

Attitude that expects success, not failure, so you will come to believe in yourself and know that you were "born to win." May you come to learn and

Know how to get along with others in order to cultivate loving relationships so necessary to one's emotional well-being. And finally, it is my sincerest hope that you will

Seek the source of greatness, power, achievement, and sucess—the living and loving God who promises unconditional love, uncompromising acceptance, and unlimited power. His loving hands can lift you out of the ashes of defeat, guide you through the tough times, and set you on the path of hope.

If you can achieve these things, then you will have the knowledge, strength, and courage to overcome the adversities life hands you—you will know that *it's always to soon to quit . . . and it's never too late to begin!*

Good luck and may God bless you.

Source Notes

Chapter One

1. Calvin Peete, "The Unlikeliest Champion," *Guideposts,* August 1984, p. 17.
2. Dale Hanson Bourke, "The Winning Ways of Mary Crowley" (interview), *Today's Christian Woman,* Summer 1983, pp. 44, 45.
3. Joe Carcione, "The Greengrocer," *Guideposts,* August 1984, p. 5.
4. Wally Amos, "The Calling Card," *Guideposts,* March 1985, p. 49.
5. Bruce Brookshire, "Characteristics of Successful People," *Timberlake Monthly,* February 1985, p. 4.

Chapter Two

1. Lewis Timberlake with Marietta Reed, *Born to Win* (Wheaton, Ill.: Tyndale House Publishers, 1986), pp. 194, 195.
2. For a more detailed discussion of self-esteem, see *Born to Win.*
3. Portions of this chapter are excerpted from chapter 2, "Anatomy of a Failure," in *Born to Win.*

Chapter Three

1. Allan C. Oggs, Sr., with Sherry Andrews, *You Gotta Have the Want-To* (Waco, Tex.: Word Books Publisher, 1987) p. 149.

Chapter Four

1. Lewis Timberlake with Marietta Reed, *Born to Win* (Wheaton, Ill.: Tyndale House Publishers, 1986), pp. 159, 160.
2. Ibid., pp. 78, 79.

Chapter Five

1. Lewis Timberlake with Marietta Reed, *Born to Win* (Wheaton, Ill.: Tyndale House Publishers, 1986), pp. 153–155.
2. Dale Hanson Bourke, "The Winning Ways of Mary Crowley" (interview), *Today's Christian Woman,* Summer 1983, p. 47.

Chapter Six

1. Lewis Timberlake with Marietta Reed, *Born to Win* (Wheaton, Ill.: Tyndale House Publishers, 1986), p. 37.
2. For a more detailed discussion of this subject, see *Born to Win.*
3. Ibid.

Chapter Seven

1. Portions of this section are taken from "Keys to Effective Communication," by Marietta Reed, *Living With Children,* Vol. 8, No. 2, April 1985, pp. 28, 29.
2. Glenn Kerfoot, *Keep It Simple: The Power of Little Words* (Fairfield, N.J.: Economics Press, Inc., 1961), pp. 2, 3.

Chapter Eight

1. Ecclesiastes 1:12–18 TLB.
2. John Edmund Haggai, *How to Win Over Worry* (Eugene, Ore.: Harvest House Publishers, 1959), p. 110.
3. Ibid., pp. 110, 111.
4. Allen Clark, *"Oh, God, I'm Dead": A Journey Back to Life* (Austin, Tex.: Texas Publishers Co., 1986), pp. 51–53.
5. Ibid., p. 92.

Bibliography

Alexander, A.L., comp., *Poems That Touch the Heart,* new enlarged edition, Garden City, N.Y.: Doubleday & Company, Inc., 1941, 1956.

Amos, Wally, "The Calling Card," *Guideposts,* March 1985, pp. 46–49.

Ballard, Dr. Robert D., *The Discovery of the Titanic,* Toronto, Ontario, Canada: Madison Press Books, 1987.

Banta, Bob, "IBM Worker Hurdles Handicaps," *Austin American-Statesman,* October 5, 1984.

Bourke, Dale Hanson, "The Winning Ways of Mary Crowley," *Today's Christian Woman,* Summer 1983, pp. 44ff.

Brookshire, Bruce, "Characteristics of Successful People," *Timberlake Monthly,* Vol. I, No. 8, February 1985, p. 4.

Carcione, Joe, "The Greengrocer," *Guideposts,* August 1984, pp. 2–5.

Clark, Allen, *"Oh, God I'm Dead": A Journey Back to Life,* Austin, Tex.: Texas Publishers Company, 1986.

Cousins, Dr. Norman, *Anatomy of an Illness as Perceived by the Patient,* New York: W. W. Norton Company, 1979.

DeMaris, Ovid, "The Other Side of Laughter; The Pain, the Gain, the Life of Steve Allen," *Parade Magazine,* May 5, 1985, pp. 4–9.

Haggai, John Edmund, *How to Win Over Worry,* Eugene Ore.: Harvest House Publishers, 1959, 1976.

Bibliography

Hillyer, Peter, "He Earned It," *Think Magazine,* No. 4, 1985, pp. 10–12.

Institute in Basic Youth Conflicts, Inc., *Character Sketches,* Vol. I, 1978.

Kerfoot, Glenn, *Keep It Simple: The Power of Little Words,* Fairfield, N.J.: Economics Press, Inc., 1961.

Minirth, Frank B., M.D., and Paul D. Meier, M.D., *Happiness Is a Choice,* Grand Rapids, Mich.: Baker Book House, 1978.

"New Lawyer Beats the Odds," *USA Today,* May 19, 1986, p. 2A.

Oggs, Allan C., with Sherry Andrews, *You Gotta Have the Want-To,* Waco, Tex.: Word Books Publishers, 1987.

Peete, Calvin, "The Unlikeliest Champion," *Guideposts,* August 1984, pp. 14–17.

Reed, Marietta, "Keys to Effective Communication," *Living With Children,* Vol. 8, No. 2, April 1985.

Selligson, Tom, "The Making of a Champion: What Debbie Reynolds Has Endured," *Parade Magazine,* May 13, 1984, pp. 4–7.

Timberlake, Lewis with Marietta Reed, *Born to Win,* Wheaton, Ill.: Tyndale House Publishers, 1986.

"W. Clement Stone On: Developing Your Natural Abilities," *PMA Adviser,* March 1985.

For information about Lewis Timberlake's seminars,
books, cassette tapes, and newsletter,
write or call:

The Timco Group, Inc.
7200 North MoPac, Suite 225
Austin, TX 78731
(512) 345–9950